AS Level for OCR

Applied ICT

Series editor:
K. Mary Reid

www.heinemann.co.uk
✓ Free online support
✓ Useful weblinks
✓ 24 hour online ordering

01865 888058

Heinemann Educational Publishers
Halley Court, Jordan Hill, Oxford OX2 8EJ
Part of Harcourt Education

Heinemann is a registered trademark of
Harcourt Education Limited

© Maggie Banks, 2005

First published 2005

10 09 08 07 06 05
10 9 8 7 6 5 4 3 2

British Library Cataloguing in Publication Data is available
from the British Library on request.

10-digit ISBN: 0 435449 97 4
13-digit ISBN: 978 0 435449 97 1

Edited by Sian Morris
Designed by Lorraine Inglis
Typeset by Thomson Digital

Original illustrations © Harcourt Education Limited, 2005

Illustrated by Thomson Digital/Tek-Art

Cover design by Wooden Ark Studio

Printed by Edelvives

Cover photo: © Zefa Images

Acknowledgements
Every effort has been made to contact copyright holders of material reproduced in this book. Any
omissions will be rectified in subsequent printings if notice is given to the publishers.

Websites
Please note that examples of websites suggested in this book were up to date at the time of writing. It
is essential for tutors to preview each site before using it to ensure that the URL is still accurate and
the content is appropriate. We suggest that tutors bookmark useful sites and consider enabling
students to access them through the school or college intranet.

Contents

Acknowledgements

The authors and publisher would like to thank the following for permission to reproduce copyright material:

The author would like to thank the Royal Artillery Museum for the use of their newsletter on page 35.

Microsoft product screen shots reprinted with permission from Microsoft Corporation.

The author and publisher would like to thank the following for permission to reproduce photographs:
BBC/page 7
Alamy/pages 10, 47
Corbis/pages 54, 71, 82
Jazzprojects.co.uk/page 33
© 2005 Google/page 104
Crown copyright material is reproduced with the permission of the Controller of HMSO:
pages 92-94/Directgov website
page 96/Department for Education and Skills
page 97/Highways Agency
pages 116, 119/National Statistics

Every effort has been made to contact copyright holders of material produced in this book. Any omissions will be rectified in subsequent printings if notice is given to the publishers.

Introduction

This is one in a series of four volumes that covers the OCR qualifications in Applied Information and Communication Technology for GCE.

The books are organised like this:

AS (Single Award), which covers units 1 to 3

AS (Double Award), which covers units 1 to 8

A2 (Single Award), which covers units 9 to 14

A2 (Double Award), which covers units 9 to 20

The two AS Level (Single and Double Award) qualifications are covered by one book each.

The two A Level (Single and Double Award) qualifications are covered by two books each, one at AS and one at A2 level.

This book covers the three units that are offered in the AS (Single Award):

Unit 1: Using ICT to communicate

Unit 2: How organisations use ICT

Unit 3: ICT solutions for individuals and society

Assessment

Your achievements on this qualification will be assessed through portfolios of evidence and an examination. The examination will be assessed externally and the portfolios will be assessed internally.

Unit 2 will be assessed externally, and you will sit a 90 minute examination, set by the examination board. You will be given a case study in advance and will be expected to do research prior to the examination itself. You will also carry out some tasks based on the case study, which you must then take into the examination. The tasks will count towards your mark for this unit.

Units 1 and 3 will be assessed internally. You will be expected to construct a portfolio for each unit. Further guidance on this is given in each unit.

Further information

You can find further information about this qualification at www.ocr.org.uk. Remember to search for GCE Applied ICT. You can download the complete specification, which gives full details of all the units, both AS and A2, and how they are assessed. This document is nearly 300 pages long.

A Tutor Resource File will provide additional material for these units.

We hope you enjoy your studies and wish you every success.

K. Mary Reid
April 2005

UNIT 1

Using ICT to communicate

Introduction

The C in ICT stands for communications. ICT has provided us with new ways to communicate information, such as email and telephone text messaging. It has also improved more traditional communication methods. For example, word processing has made it easier to produce paper-based communications, such as this book. The author can check and correct spellings and make changes without the need to rewrite or retype the text. In this unit you will learn about the different types of information, methods of communicating information and the technologies that support them.

Being able to communicate information effectively is important for both organisations and individuals. You will learn how to create effective communications that meet their purpose and the needs of their audience. You will also look at how organisations communicate and present information and understand why they use standard layouts for documents.

While you carry out your work for this unit – and all the others – you need to follow standard ways of working. This includes managing your own work, taking steps to keep information secure and working safely. What you learn in this unit will form the basis for the whole course and will provide you with skills and knowledge that will be valuable in the future, whether you continue in education or enter the world of work.

Throughout this unit and chapter, we will refer to a document, a communication, a presentation or a report. Whichever term is used, you should take it to mean any suitable way of communicating information. For example, a document does not have to be printed out on paper and a presentation does not have to be an on-screen presentation created using presentation software such as MS PowerPoint®.

How you will be assessed

This unit will be assessed on a portfolio of evidence you will provide. The Assignment Evidence at the end of this unit provides you with the ability to develop a portfolio.

What you need to learn

By studying this unit you will:

* learn about the information age: know about the characteristics and significance of different types of information, the methods used to communicate information and the technologies that support these methods of communication. You will need to be able to describe the communication methods and technologies that support them.

* be able to identify the audience for a communication, its purpose and how it will be communicated. You will be able to match the writing style you use to the communication's audience and purpose. You will need to be able to plan and create communications that use writing styles that clearly match their audience and purpose.

* be able to check the accuracy of communications and improve their readability by using spell checkers and grammar checkers and by proof-reading both content and layout. You will need to be able to use these tools effectively so that you produce final copies that contain few obvious errors.

* be capable of using a range of features and formats to create layout styles to suit the purpose of communications and that will appeal to their audience. This will include using and combining different types of media, positioning important items correctly, creating templates, creating new information and blending it with existing information and maintaining a consistent style. You will also need to evaluate the communications you produce.

* understand why and how organisations present information, the standards and layouts for formal documents, the methods of presenting a corporate image and how templates can be used to enforce corporate standards. You will need to be able to describe and compare similar documents in terms of their writing style, presentation style and their use of common standards for layout.

* be able to follow standard ways of working including managing your work effectively, keeping information secure, and working safely.

You probably already know how to use word processing software, although you may need to learn how to use some new tools and facilities. You may also need to learn how to use other types of software such as desktop publishing, presentation, multimedia authoring and web design.

The information age

How many different types of information have you received today? Reading this book you are receiving written information. You may have received audio information from your teacher (i.e. listening in class) or from the radio. Has a friend sent you a text message – again written information? If you saw an advertisement hoarding on your way to school or college, it was probably mostly graphical information. If you have been searching the World Wide Web (WWW) you will have received web-based information. This may have included words, pictures, sound and video and so becomes multimedia information or you may have been playing a computer game or using a CD-ROM. It is almost impossible not to receive information in one form or another most of our waking lives. The volume of information we receive and the different types of information have increased considerably in the last 50 or 60 years.

Types of information

Written

Written information is text based. It uses words on a page or screen to convey meaning. The words used will be part of a language and will be understood only by people who understand that language. Also, the person who is to receive the information must know how to read it. A pre-school child, for example, is unlikely to be able to receive written information because they have not yet learnt to read. An advantage of written information is that the reader can read the information at a pace that suits them. They can also backtrack and reread passages if necessary to ensure that they have understood the information. The text of this book is written information. Other examples include a text message, an email, an article in a newspaper, a note to the milkman, a letter or a memo.

> **Think it over...**
>
> When was the last time you used written information as a means of communication?

Multimedia

> **Key terms**
>
> *Multimedia*: using more than one medium to express or communicate information.
> *Media*: (singular medium) has several different but related meanings. In multimedia it means the methods by which something is expressed, communicated, or achieved, for example text, graphics, sound or video. People also refer to the media, by which they mean newspapers, television, radio, etc. In ICT we also refer to types of data storage as media, for example floppy disks and CDs to convey information.

Multimedia information, as its name suggests, uses many different types of *media*. This may include text, graphics, sound and video. Multimedia information is designed to grab the recipient's attention and make the information more interesting or entertaining than one type of information on its own. Often, when multimedia information is presented, the recipients can *interact* with the presentation, for example to choose their own paths through it. Multimedia information is used in many different ways such as entertainment, for example computer games; training and information, for example multimedia encyclopaedias.

> **Key term**
>
> *Interact*: able to select options, for example by clicking with a mouse, to affect what happens.

> **Think it over...**
>
> Can you think of three examples of multimedia communication you've encountered recently, for example ordering online?

Graphical

Graphical information is information conveyed using pictures, graphs or charts. A picture can often convey information more directly than words and may be easier to remember. Some people remember important information by imagining a picture to represent it.

An advantage of graphical information is that it is not language dependent. You do not need to understand the language of the country you are in to know which is the men's and which the women's toilet if there is a picture of a man or a woman on the door (see Figure 1.1). Similarly, it is easier to see which product provides the highest sales if the sales of the different products available are shown in a bar chart, rather than if they are simply presented as a table of figures. Road signs are another example of graphical information. We all know that a picture of a man digging means that there are roadworks ahead.

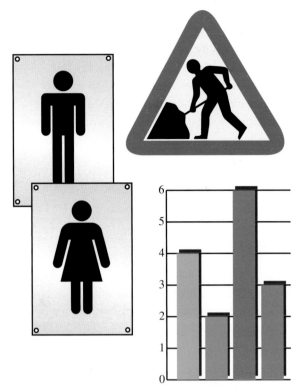

FIGURE 1.1 *Different types of graphical information understood across cultures*

Think it over...

Video clips are also used as entertainment. Can you think of any, for example Police Camera Action?

Audio

Audio information is information that we hear. This may be spoken language, in which case, the recipient needs to understand the language being used. However, the spoken word is often able to convey more information than the written word, because how something is said is frequently as meaningful as what is said. There are other forms of audio information that are not language dependent. The sound of a door-bell tells you that there is someone at the door, your computer will beep to tell you that you have hit the wrong key, a car alarm going off indicates that someone has tried to break into a car. There are many other examples of non-verbal audio information. Music, for example can convey information that we respond to in different ways (see Figure 1.2).

Video

Video information is conveyed using moving images. The images themselves may be moving or the camera recording the images may be moving or a mixture of both. Like still images, moving images convey information more directly and are more memorable than words. However, whilst a still picture supplies us with information at an instant in time and at a particular place, video information allows us to see what is happening over a period of time and/or at different places. Moving images also attract attention. There are many different uses for video information. A football manager will often look at videos of his or her team's matches to analyse the team's performance and look for ways to improve it. Close Circuit Television (CCTV) cameras provide video information to the police which helps them to detect crime and catch the people responsible. Video information about a holiday resort will give potential visitors a better idea of what the resort is like than still photographs.

FIGURE 1.2 *We can respond to music through our emotions*

Web-based

As its name suggests, web-based information is information available on the WWW. This may be written information, graphical information, video information, audio information or, indeed, multimedia information. What distinguishes web-based information is its source, its volume and its accessibility. Providing you have a computer connected to the Internet with browser software installed, you can access web-based information on almost any topic imaginable from anywhere in the world. It is also possible to access web-based information if you have a WAP (wireless application protocol) mobile phone.

Key term

Browser software: software that allows you to access and view web pages.

There are some problems associated with this volume of information and the fact that anyone can generate web-based information. It is difficult to know whether the information is accurate or simply one person's interpretation. It is also difficult, if not impossible, to police web-based information, resulting in undesirable information such as pornography or criminal information also being easily accessible.

Methods of communicating information

With so many types of information, we have gained as many, if not more methods of communicating it.

Paper-based

Computers were supposed to reduce paper-based communication and lead to a paperless office, but this is still a distant dream. Paper-based communication is anything that is written, printed, typed or drawn on paper. Both written and graphical information can be communicated on paper. This book is one example of paper-based communication but there are many others. Newspapers, letters, reports, photographs, architects' plans, examination papers and brochures are just some examples of communications that can be paper-based. An advantage of paper-based

communication, and one reason why it is still widely used, is the fact that no equipment is needed to access the information. You can read a book in bed (Figure 1.3) or on the train without the need for a computer to display the information.

FIGURE 1.3 *Reading in bed!*

Printed photographs can be put in an album and handed around for people to look at, rather than needing access to a computer to view them. It is possible to spread out an architect's plan and see the whole of it at once, rather than having to scroll around it a section at a time on-screen. Some communications, such as contracts, must be paper-based for legal reasons. It is also true that many people prefer to read from paper than from a computer screen.

Think it over...

Is this likely to change as children are brought up with screen reading?

Screen-based

It is possible to communicate video, multimedia and web-based information on screen as well as written and graphical information. Screen-based communication does not apply only to a computer screen. Television is an obvious example of screen-based communication but more and more communications in our daily lives are also screen-based. Buses, trains and even doctors' surgeries use screen-based communication to convey information. This might simply be a scrolling text message, for example listing the stations a train will stop at, or it might provide more detailed information such as the times and destinations of the next three trains to arrive at a station and whether they are on time or not.

Mobile phones can be used for screen-based communication through text and picture messaging, emails and web pages. Many people use a *PDA* to replace a diary, address book and notepad amongst other things. The information contained in the PDA is communicated on screen rather than on paper.

> **Key term**
>
> *PDA (personal digital assistant)*: a handheld computer that provides facilities for maintaining a diary, address book, notebook, etc.

SMS (short message service – telephone text messaging)

As already mentioned, mobile phones can be used for screen-based communication using text messaging. This is more correctly known as

SMS. Messages are entered using the phone's keypad and then sent to another phone with SMS capabilities. Some home phones now offer such capabilities. The main feature of SMS communications is that there is a limit on the total number of characters that can be sent in a message – hence **short** message service. To communicate as much information as possible in the number of characters available, a texting language has developed using abbreviations and numbers to convey the message. Examples are w8 = wait, 4 = for, 2 = to, tmw = tomorrow, u = you and so on. I'm sure you know many more.

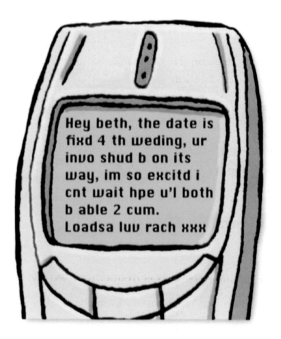

FIGURE 1.4 *How would you write this paragraph or any paragraph in this book using SMS text?*

Radio

Radio is a means of communicating audio information. Most radio is broadcast to the public on many different channels and as such it is a method of one-way communication. You can only listen to a radio broadcast. Some of these channels are local to a particular area, others are broadcast to a whole country and a few are broadcast over longer distances. There are channels that are devoted to broadcasting a particular type of music, others that are devoted to sports and others, often known as talk radio, that only broadcast the spoken word. Alongside these are channels that broadcast a range of different types of audio information. However, all radio stations will have a specific audience that they are aiming to communicate with. The advent of digital radio has provided additional channels, and radio players in web browsers enable people to listen to radio stations from the other side of the world via their computers.

> ### Key term
>
> *Frequency*: the particular waveband at which radio signals are broadcast or transmitted.

Another use of radio communication is two-way radio. This allows both parties to send and receive information. However, unlike the telephone, information can be sent in only one direction at a time. For this communication to take place, both the sending and receiving radios must be set to the same channel or *frequency*. As there is a limited band of radio frequencies, these are allocated for different uses by the government. Each broadcast radio station has its own channels, some channels are reserved for the police and other emergency services, and others for air traffic control. Citizen Band (CB) Radio is a public two-way radio service with a limited number of channels. This is frequently used by truck drivers and other motorists to communicate with each other, for example about traffic conditions. The advantage of two-way radio over mobile telephones is that the message can be received by any radio tuned to the same channel as the transmitting radio. This means that, on receipt of a 999 call, the emergency services dispatcher can broadcast the details to all vehicles, and those nearest to the scene can respond as required. Also, two-way radios often work in areas that mobile phones do not. Two-way radios may be useful for the rescue services, delivery work and security on buses.

Two-way radio is also used within a limited area, for example within a dock area for communication between staff organising the loading of vehicles onto a ferry. In these situations, there is less restriction on the frequency used because the range is too limited to cause interference with other systems.

Television

Like radio, most television is broadcast to the public and is also essentially a method of one-way communication. However, unlike radio, television communicates video as well as audio information. Like radio, there are many different channels communicating different types of information, such as sport, news, films, weather or music videos, as well as general channels that broadcast a balance of different types of information.

Digital broadcasting (see Figure 1.5) has increased the number of television channels available and has enabled viewers to interact with the programmes.

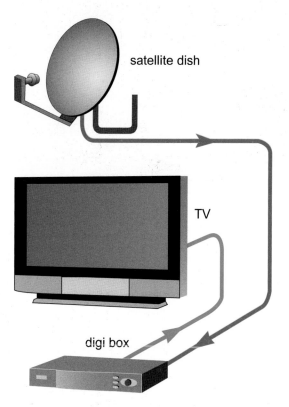

FIGURE 1.5 *Digital broadcasting*

The broadcast programmes do not use all of the available signal. There is some spare capacity that is used to transmit teletext. This consists of pages of textual information that viewers can access providing they have a television with a teletext decoder and a remote control. The viewer can access the information they require either by selecting from a series of menus or by entering the relevant page number.

Television is also used on a more local scale. This is known as close circuit television or CCTV. One of the main uses for CCTV is security. Cameras are positioned in shopping centres and other public areas as well as in and around shops, offices, banks and other buildings. The video images obtained are usually displayed on a screen that is monitored by security or other personnel. The images are also recorded so that, if anything happens, the event can be viewed again and the recordings passed to the police as evidence.

```
P100 CEEFAX 1 100 Wed 09 Jun 10:39/37
BBC CEEFAX
News
IRAQ PLAN GETS UNANIMOUS UN BACKING 104

A-Z INDEX        199  NEWS HEADLINES     101
BBC INFO         695  NEWS FOR REGION    160
CHILDREN         570  NEWSROUND          571
COOKERY          560  RADIO        BBC1  640
COMMUNITY BBC2   650  READ HEAR    BBC2  640

ENTERTAINMENT    500  SPORT              300
FILMS            540  SUBTITLING         888
FINANCE   BBC2   200  TRAVEL             430
GAMESTATION      550  TV FEATURES        520
HORSERACING      660  TV LINKS           615
LOTTERY          555  TV LISTINGS        600
MUSIC            530  WEATHER            400
  Ceefax: The world at your fingertips
Headlines  News Indx  Sport  Main Menu
```

Telephone

Traditionally, telephone has been a method of communicating audio information, but modern telephones, both mobile and landline, enable written, graphical and even video information to be communicated. The essential feature of telephone communication is that it is two-way. You can listen to what the other person is saying and you can speak to them at the same time. The increase in the use of mobile telephones has meant that people can be contacted almost anywhere when they are away from their home or place of work. It is also possible to make conference calls so that more than two people can be involved in a telephone conversation, making it possible for meetings to take place remotely.

Email

Email is written information that is communicated electronically. This is most often via a computer network, either within an organisation or the Internet, but can also be via mobile phones. With emails, it is possible to send attachments. These may be documents, pictures, video or sound files. The recipient of the email does not have to be available to receive the communication as it can be stored in an inbox and viewed later. This makes email a particularly useful method of communication between people or organisations located in different parts of the world where different time zones make telephone communication inconvenient (see Figure 1.6). It is also possible to send the same message to any number of people at the same time. However, this has led to people receiving large numbers of unsolicited, or 'junk' emails, known as spam.

FIGURE 1.6 *The difficulty of time differences!*

WWW (World Wide Web)

The WWW allows the communication of web-based information. This can be accessed using a web browser. If you know the web address (URL) of the site you want to view, this can be entered in the browser. More usually you will want to find information on a particular topic. As the amount of information available is so vast, to find the information you will need to use a search engine. You will learn more about search engines and finding web-based information in Unit 3: ICT solutions for individuals and society.

Technologies that support communication

There are many technologies that support these forms of communications.

Personal computers

Personal computers enable a number of different methods of communicating information providing they have the necessary hardware and software. All visual information will be communicated on screen, although a graphics card or video card may be needed for high-quality graphic and video information. A printer will allow you to produce paper-based communications using different types of software including word processing, desktop publishing, graphics, spreadsheet and database. A modem, cable modem, broadband modem or router and communications software will allow you to communicate using email, and a web browser will provide access to the WWW. A sound card and loudspeakers or headphones will allow you to hear audio information, and the addition of a microphone and appropriate software will allow you to communicate by telephone through your PC. We have already said that with a radio player you can listen to radio through your computer; it is also possible to have a TV adapter so that you can watch television on your computer screen as well.

Think it over...

What technologies do you need in order to send an e-card?

Touch screens

A touch screen allows people to interact with a computer without the need for a keyboard, mouse or other input device. This interaction is much more direct – instead of having to manoeuvre the mouse and then click the button, you just have to touch the relevant point on the screen. The fact that no mouse or keyboard is required also has other advantages. Less space is needed, there is less possibility of theft or vandalism and there is greater data security – without a keyboard, only the options available on screen can be accessed.

There are several different types of touch screen. The most common is known as a resistive touch screen (see Figure 1.7). This type requires you to exert a certain amount of pressure on the screen. This is because there is a plastic membrane over the screen that is separated from a glass layer by small clear dot-like spacers. The plastic and glass layers are both *conductive* but the spacers are not. When you press the screen, contact is made between the plastic and glass layers at that point so that an electrical circuit is created and a signal is sent to the computer.

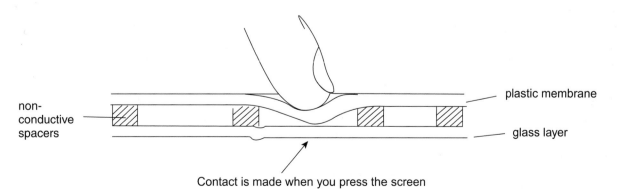

FIGURE 1.7 *Cross-section of a touch screen*

Conductive: can conduct electricity.

The other types of touch screen do not require pressure to be applied. They rely on identifying the co-ordinates of the point being touched. One of these, known as a capacitive touch screen, has a thin conductive film fused onto a glass layer, with another layer of anti-scratch glass on top of it. Electrical circuits at the corners of the screen distribute a uniform low-voltage alternating current electrical field across the conductive film. When you touch the screen, the electrical field is disrupted. The change in electrical current from each corner is measured and used to calculate the x and y co-ordinates of the point you are touching. Other types of touch screen use ultrasound or infrared to find the position of your finger.

Touch screens are particularly useful in public places where other devices might be easily damaged or take up too much space. They allow the user to make choices by touching an area on the screen to access the information they need. One example of this is in the Bullring shopping centre in Birmingham where visitors can use touch screens to find the location of a particular shop or find shops of a particular type, as well as other information. Other examples include tourist information screens and car supermarkets, where customers can use touch screens to find out what cars are available matching their requirements. Touch screens are also used on small portable devices such as PDAs. Here, because of the small size, a pointer or stylus is used to select options, rather than a finger. It is also possible to 'write' on the screen to input text and numbers.

Digital broadcasting

Key terms

Bits: binary digit, i.e. 0 or 1.
Set-top box: a box about the size of a DVD player that is connected between the satellite dish, aerial or cable input and the television set.
Bandwidth: the number of bits per second that can be transmitted.

Until the mid 1990s, most radio and television broadcasting was analogue – the picture or sound was provided by a constantly changing signal and each channel could broadcast only one programme. Since then, digital broadcasting has become more and more widely available and will eventually replace analogue broadcasting. Digital television broadcasting transmits multimedia data in much the same form as data received by a computer via the Internet – streamed *bits* of data. This data can be broadcast by satellite, cable or using terrestrial broadcasting – through an aerial that was used for receiving analogue broadcasts. The signal must then be converted back to pictures and sound (decoded), either using a *set-top box* or an integrated digital television (iDTV) where the decoder is built into the television set. Digital television provides improved quality of pictures and sound. It also allows more programmes to be transmitted over the same *bandwidth* than is possible for analogue broadcasts. This enables a television station to broadcast different versions of a sporting event taken from different camera angles, for example, allowing the viewer to select the one they want to watch. This provides viewers with some limited interaction – the viewer is merely selecting one of the many signals being broadcast, rather than sending data back to the source of the broadcast. It is also possible to broadcast a film on several different channels, starting at different times so that viewers can choose when they want to watch it. Digital television also offers truly interactive services. This can include gaming, betting, shopping, banking, email and Internet access. Where digital television is provided by satellite, this is made possible by connection to a standard telephone line. With cable services there is a built-in return path that allows such two-way communication.

Digital radio provides digital-quality sound – similar to a CD or MP3 player. However, a special digital receiver is needed to listen to it. As well as the improved sound and reception quality, it is possible to broadcast text, data and even still pictures alongside the audio signal.

DVD (digital video disk)

> **Key term**
>
> *Optical storage medium*: a disk that stores data by altering the optical characteristics of the surface material, e.g. the way light is reflected off it.

A DVD is an *optical storage medium* that can hold 4.7 Gb or more of data. This means that a DVD can store two hours of full motion video, such as a full-length feature film. As on a pre-recorded CD, the data is stored as a pattern of microscopic pits on the surface of the disk, which are read by reflecting light from a laser. The presence or absence of a pit represents the 1s and 0s that make up the digital data. DVDs can store much more data than CDs because the pits are closer together and the wavelength of the laser used to read them is shorter. Double-layered DVDs are also available. These have two parallel layers of pits at different depths. The reading laser is able to focus on each of these layers. These DVDs can hold 8.5 GB or over 4 hours of video. DVDs can be read by a DVD player, usually connected to a television, or by a DVD drive on a computer. DVD writers make it possible to store data and television programmes on DVD-R or DVD-RW disks, making magnetic videotapes and video recorders obsolete. However, DVD-R and DVD-RW use different methods of recording the data onto the blank disks.

Mobile phones

Mobile phones have transformed the way we communicate with others. Some people no longer have a landline telephone and rely exclusively on a mobile phone to keep in touch with family and friends, and for business. With mobile phones, people can be contacted anywhere there is a signal, be that in town, on the beach or even the other side of the world. Mobile phones are also known as cell phones. This is because they operate in cells. When you make a call, your phone is connected to the nearest cell via an antenna. The network is then searched to find the cell where the number you are ringing is located. When the connection is made (see Figure 1.8) the signal is sent from your phone to the nearest cell, then across the network to the receiving cell and finally from this cell to the phone you are calling and vice versa.

This means that a phone has to transmit signals only to the nearest cell. As well as voice communication, as we have already discovered, mobile phones can be used to send SMS messages.

The Internet

The Internet is a world-wide network of computer networks. It was first created in 1966 by the US government's defence research agency as a means of ensuring that there was no single 'nerve centre' in their communications

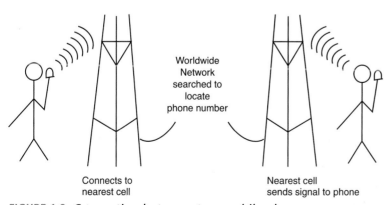

Worldwide Network searched to locate phone number

Connects to nearest cell

Nearest cell sends signal to phone

FIGURE 1.8 *Connection between two mobile phones*

network that could be wiped out by a nuclear attack. In the 1980s major university networks, for example JANET (the UK's Joint Academic Network) was connected to this network and since then it has continued to expand. Now, it connects all the major public, private and university networks. When you connect to the Internet, you connect to a network owned by an Internet Service Provider (ISP). This network is connected to others in a tree structure. The main 'trunk' of the tree that carries long-distance messages consists of a small number of high-speed, high-capacity networks known as Internet backbone networks. These are mainly the original military networks plus high-speed lines owned by major telephone companies.

It is easy to think that the Internet and the WWW are the same thing, but they are not. As we have discovered, the Internet has been in existence since the 1960s, the WWW since 1992. The WWW is only one of the services that the Internet provides. Other services provided include email, chat rooms and bulletin boards, all of which provide different ways of communicating information (see Figure 1.9).

WAP (wireless application protocol)
This is a way of sending information such as web pages to and from devices such as mobile phones. It provides a way of minimising the data sent because download speeds on mobile devices are slow compared with computers with normal connections to the Internet. Using WAP it is possible to access the WWW from a mobile phone but there will be less interactivity than would normally be available via a computer connected to the Internet.

> ## Knowledge check
>
> 1 Give one advantage and two disadvantages of written communication.
>
> 2 Describe possible problems associated with web-based information.
>
> 3 Why is paper-based communication still widely used?
>
> 4 Which methods of communication do personal computers support and how?
>
> 5 How have mobile phones and WAP changed the way we communicate?

Communication of information

So far you have learnt about different types of information and how they are communicated (summarised in Table 1.1). Now we will consider how to communicate different types of information effectively. When

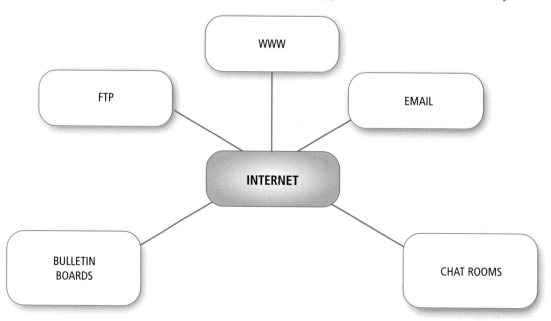

FIGURE 1.9 *Some services provided by the Internet*

TYPE OF INFORMATION	COMMUNICATION METHODS	TECHNOLOGIES
Written	Paper-based, screen-based, SMS, email, WWW	Personal computers, touch screens, mobile phones, the Internet, WAP
Multimedia	Screen-based, television, WWW	Personal computers, digital broadcasting, DVD, the Internet
Graphical	Paper-based, screen-based, WWW	Personal computers, touch screens, the Internet
Video	Screen-based, television, WWW	Personal computers, digital broadcasting, DVD, the Internet
Audio	Radio, television, telephone, WWW	Personal computers digital broadcasting, DVD, the Internet
Web-based	WWW	The Internet, WAP

TABLE 1.1 *How types of information, communication methods and technologies are linked*

you want to communicate some information, there are three questions you need to ask yourself.

1 Who is going to receive it – who will be the audience?

2 What is the communication's purpose?

3 What method will be used to communicate the information?

By answering these questions it will help you to decide on the style of language to use. If you are writing a note to a friend you will use informal language, as informal purposes demand an informal style; if you are writing a letter to apply for a job you will need to use formal language, as formal purposes demand a formal style (see Figure 1.10).

A presentation for young children will need to use short words and simple sentence constructions; a business *report* will use more complex words and sentences.

> **Key term**
>
> *Report*: a long document that presents the results of some research or the activities an organisation has undertaken during the previous year and its financial position.

Room 354, Block 6
Model Village
North Point
Hong Kong
Phone: 24862893
Mobile: 95427415
E-mail: wwm654@hkinternet.com
13 July 2005

Mr William Chan
Personnel Manager
XYZ Consulting
PO Box 583
Kwai Chung
Kowloon

Dear Mr Chan

Application for the Post of Management Trainee

I am writing to apply for the post of Management Trainee, which was advertised on the Student Affairs Office notice board of the Hong Kong Polytechnic University on 13 July 2005.

My working experience at Lucky Star Garment Manufactory Limited improved my leadership skills, communication skills and ability to work in a team environment. I have fluent spoken and written English. I also have fluent spoken and written Mandarin, and can therefore work in mainland China.

Currently I am studying a B.A. in Management at the Hong Kong Polytechnic University, graduating in 2006.

Subjects, which I am studying that are relevant to the post of Management Trainee include Operations Management, Human Resources Management, Accounting, Marketing and Strategic Management.

My final year project is entitled Knowledge Management Practices in HK. Carrying out this project has improved my communication skills, my leadership skills and my ability to lead and supervise subordinates effectively. I have also learnt how to run a project from the planning stage to its completion.

During my studies, I have held the post of Executive in the Management Society. While leading and organising Management Society activities, I have

FIGURE 1.10 *An example of a formal type of communication*

You will need to be able to use different writing styles to meet different purposes and document structures.

Attracting attention

If the purpose of a communication is to attract attention, you will need to use short punchy sentences that grab the reader's attention. An example might be 'Grand sale starts tomorrow. Don't miss the bargains.'

Think it over...

Compare two examples. What's good and bad and what improvements would you make?

Setting out facts clearly

When it is important to communicate facts clearly, you will need to use straightforward language that is easy to understand with no unnecessary descriptive words. For example, if you need to give someone directions you might write 'Leave the clockwise M25 at junction 1b (Dartford). At the top of the slip road take the third exit from the roundabout, immediately after the petrol station. Turn left at the next roundabout. The school entrance is on your right after 100 metres.'

Writing to impress

Sometimes you will need to write to impress your reader. This will give you the opportunity to use unusual words and more complex sentence structures. For example, in a job application you might write 'During the last ten years I have undertaken a plethora of responsibilities with consummate ease, enhancing my position and standing within this organisation. However, I feel I have now reached the pinnacle of the opportunities available and require new challenges.'

Summarising information

When you are summarising information, the purpose is to communicate the important points so that your audience can easily grasp them. Short bullet-pointed statements are often the best way to do this. For example, 'This unit requires you to study the following topics:

* the information age
* communication of information
* accuracy and readability
* styles of presentation

* how organisations present information
* standard ways of working.'

Creating a questionnaire

If you are creating a *questionnaire* a or if you are collecting information from individuals, you need to choose the questions you ask very carefully so that you get the response you need. Questions such as 'What do you like best about this brand of crisps?' are called open questions. If you asked 100 people, you could get 100 different responses. That would not be of much use to you if you want to do any analysis of the information you collect.

Key term

Questionnaire: a document designed to gather information and opinions from large numbers of individuals, often as part of a survey or to gain feedback on services provided.

Questions like 'Have you ever bought this brand of crisps?' are called closed questions. There are only two possible answers, yes and no. You can also ask questions that have a limited range of responses, for example 'Which of these is your favourite flavour?' with possible responses of 'cheese and onion', 'salt and vinegar', 'beef' and 'plain'. Closed and limited-response questions will help you to collect information that can be usefully analysed.

Collecting information from individuals

If you are creating a form to collect information from individuals, such as an application or booking form, you will need to ensure that it is clear what information is required. Some information may only require a simple prompt, for example 'Surname', 'Date of birth', 'Postcode', as everyone will know what is required. To obtain more complex information you may need to ask a question or write a statement to describe what is required. Some application forms have separate instructions on how to fill them in, for example an application for a passport or driving licence.

Explaining technical details

When you need to explain technical details it is important that your language is clear and accurate and that you use appropriate technical terms. For example, 'A digital television (DTV) broadcast has a 19.4 Mbit/s bandwidth. A standard DTV programme can use as few as 4.5 Mbit/s. This allows broadcasters to transmit more than one programme within a single 19.4 Mbit stream.'

Writing a reminder

A reminder is an informal document, possibly a hand-written note, a memo or an email. When you write a reminder it will be in an informal style. For example, 'Don't forget the meeting tomorrow at 2 o'clock. We're going to meet in the Sun Rise for a bite to eat, if you want to join us. We'll be there at about 1.'

Preparing a report

A report, on the other hand, is a formal document that needs a formal style. There are many different types of report but they all need to use formal language and be well structured.

Many businesses will produce an annual report for their shareholders and other interested people (see Figure 1.11). This will explain what has happened in the business in the previous year and include financial information such as the amount of money that has passed through the business and their profits for the year.

Ordering or invoicing goods

The most important consideration when creating orders and *invoices* is that they are accurate. If an incorrect address is given on an order, the goods will not get to the right place. An incorrect total on an invoice may lead to an irate customer or a loss of profit, as well as damaging the reputation of the company and losing the respect of its customers.

> **Key term**
>
> *Invoices*: A document that lists the products or services purchased from an organisation together with the cost of each, any additional costs such as carriage, the VAT due and the total amount to be paid.

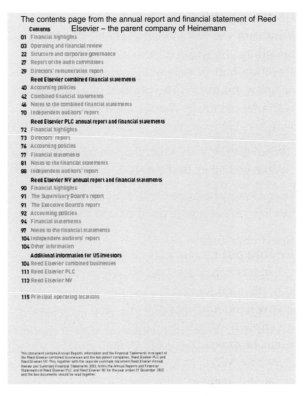

FIGURE 1.11 *The contents page from the annual report and financial statement for Reed Elsevier*

Orders and invoices may also include the terms and conditions under which the goods are supplied and payment made. The wording of these sections must be in a formal style, clear and precise, as they form part of a legal agreement between the supplier of the goods and the person buying them.

> **Think it over...**
>
> Technically explain how to open and close a file. Make sure each step is listed. Provide visual guidance.

Accuracy and readability

Some recent research has suggested that we can make sense of words, regardless of the order the letters are in, providing the first and last letters are correct.

'The rset can be a taotl mses and you can sitll raed it wouthit a porbelm.'

However, this does not make for easy reading. Imagine if you had to read a whole page like that. Inaccurate information, such as incorrect spellings, punctuation and grammar can mislead or annoy the reader. The position of a comma, for example, can totally change the meaning of a sentence. For example:

'When getting in the boat, shoes must be taken off.'
'When getting in, the boat shoes must be taken off.'

There was a court case involving a woman who lost her job because of an ill-placed comma!

Spell checkers

ICT provides us with tools to improve the accuracy of what we write. A spell checker will help you to check and correct punctuation and the spelling of words, and will also pick up repeated words, such as 'the the'. However, a spell checker only compares the words you type with an in-built dictionary. If you type 'form' when you mean 'from', or 'manger' when you mean 'manager', the spell checker will not identify these as errors. On the other hand, you may type a name, such as 'Agnew', which you know is correct, but the spell checker identifies it as an error. This is because 'Agnew' is not in the dictionary (see Figure 1.12).

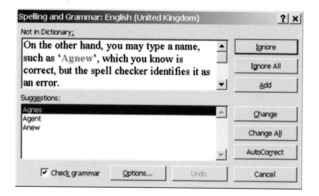

FIGURE 1.12 *Spell check*

If you use a lot of unusual words or proper names, you can create your own personal dictionary containing these words. You should not become over-reliant and expect the spell checker to spell for you. It will often provide a list of alternative spellings – you need to know which one to select. Sometimes the correct word may not be in the list or the spell checker cannot offer any

suggestions so you will need to correct the word yourself. Also, remember that the spell checker may be configured not to check certain words, such as those in capital letters, and does not tell you when you have omitted a capital letter at the start of a sentence.

> ✱ REMEMBER!
>
> Check that the spell checker is using English (UK) spellings. Quite often the spell checker is set to use US spelling, which does differ from English accepted grammar, punctuation and spelling conventions.

Grammar checker

Grammar checkers are also available to improve the accuracy of your documents. Grammar checkers compare what you type with a set of rules. You can choose which set of rules to use by selecting the style of language that you want, such as formal or technical.

A grammar checker will help you make sure that there is a capital letter to start a sentence and only one full stop at the end of it. It will also indicate if you have a single subject but a plural verb, for example 'they is', or vice versa. Also, common errors can be avoided, like writing 'you and I' when it should be 'you and me'. A useful tool of grammar checkers is to indicate where you have used the passive rather than the active voice. The passive voice is where the object of the sentence comes first, for example:

'The play was enjoyed by the audience.'

The active voice is when the subject of the sentence comes first, for example:

'The audience enjoyed the play.'

The active voice is much easier to read and has a more direct effect than the passive voice.

Grammar checkers can also provide you with readability statistics (see Figure 1.13). These will help you to meet the needs of your audience.

You need to take great care when using a grammar checker. Do not be too hasty to accept the changes suggested. Not all the changes

Theory into practice

– Selecting language style

Select *Options* in the *Tools* menu and then select the *Spelling & Grammar* tab. This dialogue box allows you to alter how the software checks spelling and grammar. In the grammar section there is a drop-down list to select the writing style. There is also a button labelled *Settings*. This takes you to another dialogue that indicates what will be checked – try changing the writing style and watch how the items selected in this list change. You can also set up your own customised writing style by selecting and deselecting these items. When you are happy, select *OK* to go back to the main dialogue box. There is a button that allows you to recheck your document. Try selecting different writing styles and options to see the effect on your documents.

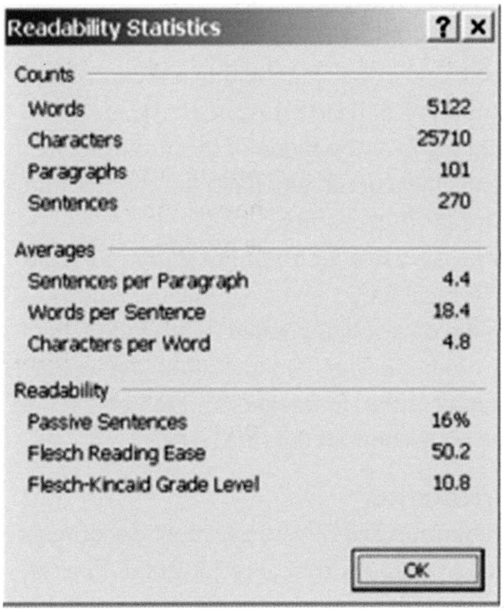
Readability Statistics
? ×
Counts
Words 5122
Characters 25710
Paragraphs 101
Sentences 270
Averages
Sentences per Paragraph 4.4
Words per Sentence 18.4
Characters per Word 4.8
Readability
Passive Sentences 16%
Flesch Reading Ease 50.2
Flesch-Kincaid Grade Level 10.8
OK

FIGURE 1.13 *Readability*

suggested improve the grammar of a sentence – some might change the meaning or make it meaningless.

Proof-reading

As you have already discovered, spelling and grammar checkers will not identify and correct all the errors you might make. It is very important that you proof-read your work. This means that you should read it through carefully to check for errors that the spelling and grammar checkers have not picked up. You should also check that what you have written makes sense, meets your purpose, and that the layout is correct. It is good practice to proof-read and correct errors on screen before you print the document. However, layout errors may not be evident until you print the work out. It is also often easier to spot errors on paper than on screen, so always give the printed copy a final check.

✱ REMEMBER!

The language used to convey information depends on:

* the audience
* the purpose
* the method of communication.

The accuracy of the information conveyed is important.

Software provides tools such as spelling and grammar checkers but these are no substitute for careful proof-reading.

Styles of presentation

How you present information is as important to your audience as the style of language you use and the accuracy of the content. Different font styles and sizes may help to differentiate between headings and the main body of a communication, or pick out a particular passage in the text, but use too many and the effect becomes confusing and annoying. Inconsistent headings and layout are common mistakes. When you are preparing a communication you need to think carefully about how you will present it to achieve the right impact and appeal to your audience.

In the following sections you will learn about the features that affect presentation style and how to use or modify them to suit your purpose.

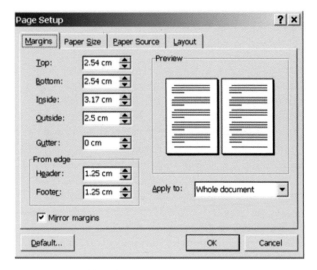

FIGURE 1.14 *Margins*

Margins are often blank, but books sometimes have wide side margins to contain marginal comments, and the top and bottom margins of many documents contain headers and footers.

Headers and footers

A header is text that lies within the top margin and that appears on every page within a section of the document. Typical header text might be the document's title or the name of the author. Long documents like a book may have the chapter title in the header for that chapter.

A footer is like a header but it lies within the bottom margin. Typical footer text might be the page number, the date it was created or amended, the version number or the filename of the document. You can have different headers and footers on odd and even pages and on the first page.

Page orientation

Page orientation arises because most documents are printed on paper that is rectangular. Portrait orientation is when the text is printed parallel to the narrow edge of the paper. Landscape orientation is when the text is printed parallel to the long edge of the paper (see Figures 15A and B). You need to consider carefully which orientation you should use for each communication you create. Business letters are always printed portrait, as are most books, brochures and newsletters. However, within these, a table, picture or chart that is wider than it is high may be printed landscape.

Page layout

Page layout features usually relate to how information is presented on the printed page. These features can be set up or modified in word processing or desktop publishing software to achieve the required layout.

Margins

Margins are the spaces between the edge of the text and the edge of the page. You can set the width of the top, bottom, left and right margins (see Figure 1.14). If you are creating a letter, the left and right margins would usually be the same but you might need to increase the size of the top margin if the letter is to be printed on headed notepaper. Reducing the size of margins is a useful trick if you are trying to fit a table, for example, on one page. If you are producing a longer document that is going to be printed on both sides of the paper and then hole-punched or bound, you would need a wider margin on the inside edge of each page. This would be the left margin on odd pages and the right one on even pages. You can set the software to 'mirror' the margins to achieve this effect.

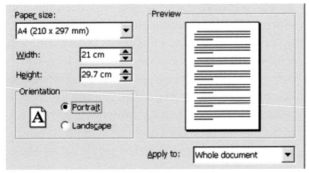
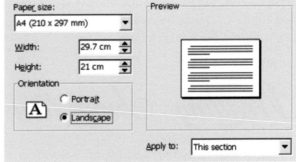

FIGURE 1.15A–B *Orientation can be portrait (1.15A) or landscape (1.15B) and applied to the whole document or part of it*

More informal documents, such as advertisements or an invitation, may be printed landscape but, in general, portrait is the more commonly used orientation.

Paper size

There are many different sizes of paper. In the USA, letter (8.5″ wide by 11″ high), legal (8.5″ by 14″) and executive (7.25″ by 10.5″) are used but in the UK the most commonly used paper size in business is A4. A4 paper is 21 cm wide and 29.7 cm high – 8.27″ by 11.69″. A4 is one of a series of paper sizes, all of which are exactly half the size of the previous one in the series. So, A4 is half the size of A3, which itself is half the size of A2, and if you fold a piece of A4 paper in half you get A5 (see Figure 1.16).

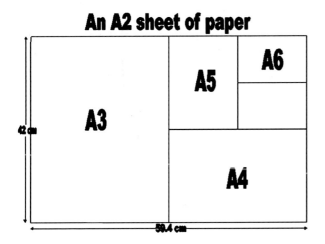

FIGURE 1.16 *Paper sizes*

This means you can create an A5 booklet by printing the pages landscape on A4 paper and folding them in half.

Pagination

Pagination is how text is distributed between the pages of a multi-page document. Software will automatically move text onto a new page when the previous one is full, but you can force text onto a new page before then by inserting a manual page break. You can also adjust where automatic page breaks occur to prevent *widows* and *orphans*. Remember this applies only to a paragraph, so you may need to manually insert a page break to keep a heading with the paragraph it relates to.

Key terms

Widow: where the first line of a paragraph is left on its own at the bottom of a page.
Orphan: where the last line of a paragraph ends up on its own at the top of a new page.

Gutters

The blank extra margin on the inside edge of pages that will be bound is called a gutter. This will be within the binding when the pages are bound.

Textual styles

Fonts

As you learnt at the beginning of this section, the use of too many different font styles and sizes can be confusing and annoying but careful selection and use of these can enhance your presentation style. There are many different font styles available in many different sizes. The font style and size you use for your communication will depend on its purpose and audience. A fancy font (see Figure 1.17) may be suitable for an invitation to a wedding but not for a business letter.

Wedding Invitation

FIGURE 1.17 *A fancy font suitable for a wedding invitation*

Many business documents will use a font style like the one used for this book – Times New Roman. This is known as a serif font. Others will use a sans serif font style such as **Arial**.

> ✱ REMEMBER!
>
> Arial, Verdana and Helvetica are conventionally used for web pages.

If you look at letters such as the i, r and l carefully, you will see how these two families of fonts differ. The letters in the serif font have short strokes – called serifs – that are missing from sans serif fonts – sans means without in French. It is considered easier to read serif fonts because the serifs draw your eye along to the next letter.

The font size you use is also important. This too will depend on the purpose of your communication and your audience. If you are creating an on-screen presentation to show to an audience, you will probably need to use a font size of at least 20 point. A book for young children may use a 14 pt font size, but for most business letters, reports and other formal documents, you should use a font size between 10 and 12 pt. Font sizes smaller than 10 pt can be difficult to read. Information that must be included in a communication for legal reasons is often printed in a small font size so that the reader's attention is not drawn to it. Such information is often known as 'the small print'.

Headings and title styles
Headings and titles give a communication structure and help the reader to know what each section is about. There may be main headings and different levels of sub-headings to break the text up further, as shown in this book. If each different level of title or heading has its own style, it will help the reader to recognise which level a heading belongs to. It is important that you use title and heading styles consistently. Software will help you to do this by allowing you to set named styles. For example, you could create a style called Main Heading that is Times New Roman 18 pt, bold. Every time you need a main heading, you would only need to select this style.

> **Theory into practice**
>
> – setting heading styles
>
> Select *Style* from the *Format* menu. Next select the *New* button. Type in a name for your style and then click on the *Format* button. You will be given different formatting options such as *Font* and *Paragraph*. Change the formatting to what you want for this style then click on *OK* to return to the previous dialogue box. When you have made all the changes, click *Apply* on the main *Style* dialogue.

Bold, italic and underline
Bold, *italic* and <u>underline</u> are all ways of drawing attention to particular words or sections of text. They are effective only if you use them sparingly. Underline is now commonly used to indicate a *hyperlink*. It is not normally used for headings except in hand-written documents. Emboldening the most important word in a phrase or sentence will make it stand out and grab the reader's attention. Italics are also commonly used for emphasis but, if a whole document is in italics, it just becomes more difficult to read. Titles and heading styles often use bold to make them stand out.

> **Key term**
>
> *Hyperlink*: an area of an on-screen document or presentation that takes the user to another part of the presentation or to a different location, such as another file or a web page, when it is clicked on.

Superscript and subscript

Usually, letters appear on an imaginary line, with only the 'tails' of letters like g or p below it. Sometimes you may need letters to appear above the line, for examplest 1st. The 'st' is in superscript – MS Word will do this automatically but you can switch this feature off. Similarly, if you want to type the chemical formula for water, H_2O, the 2 needs to be below the line,- or in subscript. This is achieved by highlighting the 2 and then checking subscript in the Format Font dialogue (see Figure 1.18).

Text orientation

Most text you type will appear horizontally on the page, like this does. However, if the text is in a frame, it is possible to change the orientation of some of the text on the page so that it appears vertically on the page.

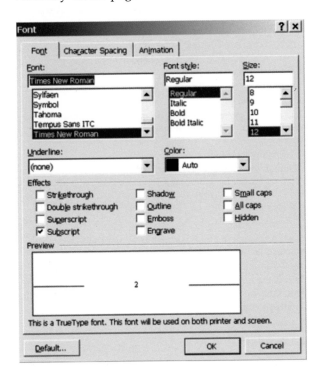

FIGURE 1.18 *Subscript*

Text animation (on-screen)

If you are producing an on-screen communication, you can also animate the text (see Figure 1.19). This can either be how it arrives on the screen, such as letter by letter or word by word, or how it appears, such as a flashing background or moving border. Both text orientation and text animation should be used only for effect and sparingly so that the reader does not become confused or distracted.

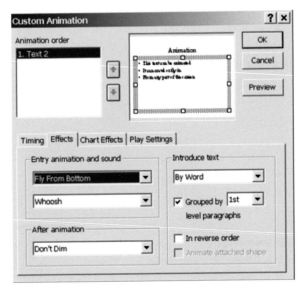

FIGURE 1.19 *Animating text in a slide presentation*

Paragraph formats

There are a number of options available that allow you to control how the text within a communication is set out in paragraphs.

Tabs and indents

A tab allows you to move the typing cursor to a certain distance along the line. You can set tabs at different positions on the line and every time you press the **Tab** key, the cursor will move to the next position. Tabs are usually used with individual items in a list to ensure that each starts at the same distance from the margin. The standard tab setting starts the word at the tab position – it is left aligned. It is also possible to set tabs that are centre aligned, right aligned, or decimal aligned. The last of these is used for columns of figures so that the decimal points are all under one another.

	23.4
	361.35
	3.671
Total	388.421

Another feature of tabs are the leaders. These give a line of dots, dashes or a solid line leading to the tab position. For example:

Item 1 ....Page 24
Item 2 ....Page 139

This is an example of a right aligned tab with leader dots.

Theory into practice

– setting tabs

Select *Tabs* from the *Format* menu. Type in a tab position and select the tab alignment and any leader by clicking the radio buttons. Don't forget to click on the *Set* button to set each tab, which will be used within the document from then on.To clear a tab, select it in the list and then click the *Clear* button. Experiment with different combinations of tab positions, alignments and leaders.

An indent is usually used with paragraphs of continuous text. If you set an indent, you can make every line in a paragraph start and finish a set distance in from the margins. This is often used when a quotation is included in a document to differentiate it from the rest of the text. This paragraph has left and right indents of 1 cm.

A first line indent is when only the first line starts at the set distance from the left margin. First line indents used to be used to indicate a new paragraph but a blank line is usually used for this purpose now. This paragraph has a 1 cm first line indent.

With a hanging indent, the first line starts at the left margin and the rest of the paragraph is indented. This is mostly used with bullets or numbering. This paragraph has a 1 cm hanging indent.

Paragraph numbering

The paragraphs within a document can be numbered. In a long document such as a report, multi-level numbering may be used. The main sections in the document may be numbered 1, 2, 3, etc., sub-sections may be numbered 1.1, 1.2, 1.3, etc. and these sections may also have sub-sections numbered 1.1.1, 1.1.2, 1.1.3, and so on (see Figure 1.20).

1 Customers

1.1 Shops

1.1.1 High Street

The number of customers buying from our high street shops this Christmas has shown a marked decline over previous years.

1.1.2 Shopping Malls

Although the reduction in customer numbers has not been as great as for our high street outlets, there has still been some reduction from last year.

1.2 Remote

1.2.1 Mail Order

Customer numbers from our mail order catalogue has seen some reduction this year.

1.2.2 The Internet

This is the main growth area. Customer numbers have more than doubled since last Christmas.

2 Suppliers

2.1 UK-based

2.2 Overseas

FIGURE 1.20 *Multi-level numbering*

Such numbering makes it possible for a reader to refer accurately to a particular part of the report. Numbering is also used to indicate points or actions that are in a specific order, for example in recipes and instructions.

Widows and orphans

As you learned on page 19, widows and orphans are where the first or last line of a paragraph is on a different page from the rest of the paragraph. The automatic page breaks can be set to avoid widows and orphans.

Theory into practice

– preventing widows and orphans

Select *Paragraph* in the *Format* menu and then the *Line and Page Breaks* tab. Checking the *Widows/Orphans control* box will ensure that these are avoided.

Alignment

A paragraph that has a straight left edge and a jagged right edge is left aligned. If the left edge is jagged and the right edge is straight, the paragraph is right aligned. Centre alignment is where each line starts and ends the same distance from its centre. If a paragraph is justified, both left and right edges are straight. The spaces between words are extended as necessary (see Figure 1.21 for examples of alignment).

A paragraph that has a straight left edge and a jagged right edge is *left aligned*.

If the left edge is jagged and the right edge is straight, the paragraph is *right aligned*.

Centre alignment is where each line starts and ends the same distance from its centre.

If a paragraph is *justified*, both left and right edges are straight. The spaces between words are extended as necessary.

FIGURE 1.21 *Alignment*

Left alignment is commonly used for many types of document. Right alignment may be used to align an address on the right margin of a letter, for example. Centre alignment may be used for headings or for communications such as greetings cards, menus, posters or flyers with limited text.

Newspapers and newsletters use justified paragraphs. Justified paragraphs are also used in business letters that use a style called 'fully blocked'.

Spacing before/after

Adding space before or after a paragraph is useful when you want some space but not a whole line between a heading and the following paragraph or before a bullet list. You can specify the point size of the space you want to leave. Adding spacing before and after items in a table provides some white space between the text and the borders of the cells. These options can be found in the **Format Paragraph** dialogue box.

Use of tables

Tables help to organise information on the page or screen. You can use a table rather than tabs to align columns of short items. If you do not add borders to the table, the effect will be exactly the same. However, with a table, each item can extend onto more than one line. Table 1.2 shows the flight details for a trip to Australia. A 3 pt space has been added before and after each paragraph to move the text away from the borders making it easier to read. The cells in the first and fifth rows have been merged to allow each heading to appear on one line and to differentiate them from the details.

Bullet points

Bullet points are similar to numbered paragraphs but are used to identify a list of points that are in no particular order.

Line spacing

It is possible to adjust the space between the lines within a paragraph. Line spacing within a paragraph is most commonly single, 1.5 or double, relating to the font size being used. However, you can set the line spacing to be at least a set point size or exactly a set point size, or larger multiples of the font size such as 2.5 or 3 times. Many documents use single line spacing, but adding extra space between the lines may make the text easier to read. Double line spacing is often used for the draft copy of a document as it allows space to annotate the text with suggested changes and comments.

FLIGHT DETAILS – OUTBOUND					
AIRLINE	**FLIGHT NO.**	**DEPARTURE AIRPORT AND TERMINAL**	**DESTINATION**	**DEPARTING**	**ARRIVING**
Malaysia Airlines	0003	London Heathrow Terminal 3	Kuala Lumpur	28/03/05 1200	29/03/05 0730
Malaysia Airlines	0129	Kuala Lumpur	Melbourne Victoria	29/03/05 0950	29/03/05 2030
FLIGHT DETAILS – INBOUND					
AIRLINE	**FLIGHT NO.**	**DEPARTURE AIRPORT AND TERMINAL**	**DESTINATION**	**DEPARTING**	**ARRIVING**
Malaysia Airlines	0148	Melbourne Victoria Terminal 1	Kuala Lumpur	28/04/05 1540	28/04/05 2030
Malaysia Airlines	0002	Kuala Lumpur	London Heathrow	29/04/05 2340	29/04/05 0550

TABLE 1.2

Hyphenation

Hyphenation allows a long word that will not fit on the current line to be split and a hyphen inserted. You can switch hyphenation off so that words are not split in this way.

Special features

There are a number of special features you need to be able to use to develop special presentation styles.

Borders

You can use borders around paragraphs as well as in tables. A border around a paragraph will make it stand out from the rest of the text and draw the reader's attention to it.

Shading

Shading behind the text can also draw attention to it. However, you need to be careful that the shading is not too dark, so that the text can still be read easily.

Background and text colour

For screen-based communications, or those that will be printed in colour, you can select the colour of the background and the text colour. You need to be careful which colours you choose to use together. For example, if you use red text on a green background, it will be unreadable by anyone who is red-green colour blind. You should also limit the number of different colours you use (see Figure 1.22). A rainbow of different colours is likely to annoy the audience and distract them from the information you are trying to communicate.

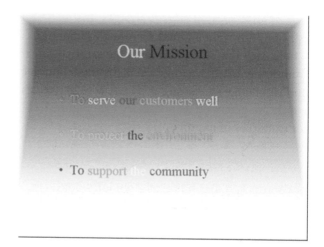

FIGURE 1.22 *Too many colours have been used on this page*

A contents page

A contents page is an important feature of a multi-page document. It should list the main sections of the document with their page numbers. If you use named heading styles, you can make the word processing software create a contents page automatically (see Figure 1.23).

Theory into practice

Check the contents page of this book.

– creating a contents page

Before you can create a table of contents, you must have set up and used named heading styles in your document. Select *Index and Tables* from the *Insert* menu and select the *Table of Contents* tab.

You can select different pre-set formats for the contents table, whether to include page numbers, whether these should be right aligned and whether to include a leader or not. You can also select how many levels of heading should be listed in the table of contents. Clicking the *Options* button will enable you to select the named style you have used and the level of each. The *Modify* button will allow you to change the style of each level of heading in the table of contents.

index lists important words in alphabetical order, along with the pages each word appears on. You can mark the words you want to appear in an index, and the word processing software will create the index for you – this is also done using the **Index and Tables** dialogue box.

Try this on a document you've already created.

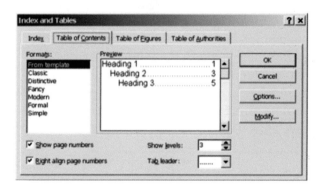

FIGURE 1.23 *Creating a table of contents*

An index

An index is also a feature of longer documents. You will find one at the end of this book. The

A bibliography

A bibliography lists all the sources of information you use when creating a communication. You will need to create a bibliography to list all the sources of information that you use when you are producing the assessment evidence for this unit. The purpose of a bibliography is to allow someone else to find the same information as you did. You must provide enough information for them to do so. For a book, you should list the name of the author(s), the title and the publisher as a minimum (see Table 1.3). A formal bibliography will also state where and when the book was published. If you use information from a web page you should list the exact URL of the page you used. If you use a magazine or other publication, you will need to list its title, publisher and the date it was issued (and/or the volume number and issue number).

Bessant, A	Learning to Use Your Computer	Heinemann	Dec 2002	ISBN 0435455478
de Watteville, A & Gilbert L	AVCE ICT Student Book 2nd Edition	Heinemann	Oct 2000	ISBN 0435453076
http://www.io.com/~hcexres/tcm1603/acchtml/genlett.html				
http://esl.about.com/cs/onthejobenglish/a/a_basbletter.htm				
http://www.textmatters.com/tm/guides/dbd.html				

TABLE 1.3 *Part of a bibliography*

An appendix

Information that you want to refer to but that you do not want to include in the main body of the document should be put in an *appendix* at the end of the document. You should clearly number each appendix, e.g. Appendix 1, Appendix 2, and refer to them in the main document, for example 'see the sales figures in Appendix 1'. If no reference is made to an appendix, it should not be included.

> **Key term**
>
> *Appendix*: numbered sections at the end of a document that contain relevant information that is referred to in the document but does not form part of it.

Text/picture boxes

Text and picture boxes allow you to position a picture or some text where you want it to appear on the page or screen. You can then choose how you want the rest of the text to wrap around it. Desktop publishing software uses text and picture boxes (or frames – see Figure 1.24) to hold and position all text and pictures.

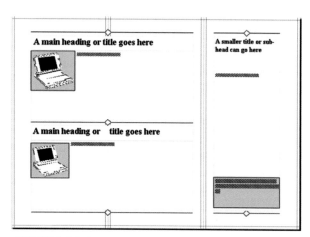

FIGURE 1.24 *Frames*

Types of media

Much of what we have looked at so far relates to presenting textual information. We have already said that graphical information is more direct and memorable than written information. So, many types of presentation can be improved by incorporating various types of media such as different types of graphics, charts, video clips and sound.

Graphs or charts

If you have to communicate numerical information, a graph or chart may make it easier for your audience to understand than a table or list of figures. For example, a line graph is often used to show the variation in temperature in a holiday resort for different months of the year. You could use a pie chart to show the proportion of boys and girls studying ICT in your school or college, or a bar chart to show the number of boys and girls taking each subject. Do be careful, however, that you choose the correct type of graph for the data you need to display.

Lines or borders

Lines and borders are effective ways to visually break a page or screen up into separate areas. You can use a horizontal line below the title on each slide of a slide presentation, or above the footer on a printed document. You can place a vertical line between the columns of a two or three-column newsletter to help guide the reader's eye down each column or put a border around an article to draw attention to it (see Figure 1.25).

FIGURE 1.25 *Vertical lines between columns*

Video clips

On-screen communications such as multimedia presentations and web pages allow you to include video clips and sound to liven up the presentation and attract the audience's attention. For example, if you are producing a multimedia presentation about your local area for the tourist office, including a video clip will give people a better idea of what the area is like than still photos alone.

Pictures

There are a number of different types of graphic images that you can include to improve presentation style. These include:

* pictures created using painting packages (*bitmap* images)

* line drawings created using *vector graphic* packages

* photographs taken with a digital camera can be imported directly into your presentation

* photographs taken with a digital camera that can be imported directly into your presentation

* extensive libraries of clipart images can illustrate the information you are trying to convey

* scanned images such as printed photographs can be imported.

One point to bear in mind, however, is that whichever images you use they must be appropriate to the purpose of the communication and the needs of your audience.

Sound

Sound can make a presentation more accessible as well as attracting attention. Spoken instructions can be recorded and added to the presentation or the text of the presentation can be read aloud and recorded. Both of these additions would help a young child or a person who is visually impaired to access the presentation. Other types of sound such as music or sound effects can also be used effectively.

Positioning important items

Addressee details, dates, logos, signatures and headings should follow standard layouts (see Figure 1.26).

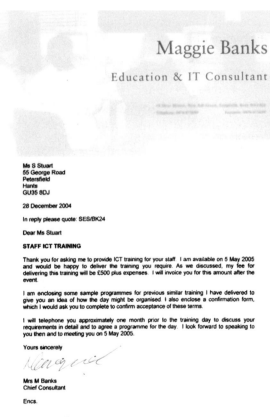

FIGURE 1.26 *A business letter*

There are standard conventions for the layout of some documents such as business letters. A reference and the date are positioned above the main body of the letter, as are the name and address of the person being written to – the addressee. One reason for this is to allow the use of 'window' envelopes. Conventionally used in business, these are envelopes that have a see-through window that allows the name and address to be seen and which does away with the need to write or print the address on the envelope. Business letters often include a heading to indicate what the letter is about. This is positioned at the beginning of the letter below the salutation (the Dear …). Space needs to be left for a signature at the end of the letter. This will come after the complimentary close (Yours faithfully or Yours sincerely). The person's name and their position are usually printed below their signature. Many organisations will also have their own rules for positioning items such as the company logo as part of their house style. We will look at house style in more detail in the section about how organisations present information.

✳ REMEMBER!

There are many different features that affect the style of a presentation. The features you use will depend on the purpose of your communication, what you want to achieve with it and what will appeal to your audience. These features apply to:

✳ page layouts – margins, headers and footers, page orientation, paper size, pagination and gutters

✳ textual style – fonts, headings and title styles, bold, italic and underline, superscript and subscript, text orientation and text animation

✳ paragraph formats – tabs and indents, paragraph numbering, widows and orphans, justification, spacing before/after, use of tables, bullet points, line spacing and hyphenation

✳ special features – use of borders, use of shading, background colour, text colour, a contents page, an index, a bibliography, an appendix and text/picture boxes

✳ types of media – graphs or charts, lines or borders, video clips, pictures, drawings, digital photographs, clip art, scanned images and sound

✳ position of important items – references, signatures, dates, logos, addressee names and headings.

Creating communications

So far you have learnt about the different writing and presentation techniques that you can use to create different types of communications. You will need to learn to judge when to use different techniques to match the purpose and audience for each communication.

How to create templates to standardise styles of presentation

Templates will help you to create a standardised presentation style. A template allows you to set

Theory into practice

– creating and using a template

Open a new document, set the page layout and any textual styles. Type in any standard text that will appear on every document and import any graphics such as a logo. Instead of just clicking the *Save* button, select *Save As* from the file menu. Type in a name for the template and then select *Document Template (*.dot)* from the *Save As Type* drop-down list. Click the *Save* button. To use the template, select *New* from the *File* menu, then select your template and click *OK*.

things like the style and size of fonts and the position of items so that these are the same every time you use the template.

When to use existing information
There is a saying 'Why re-invent the wheel?' Sometimes, the information you want to communicate already exists. It may be better to use the existing information than to try to recreate it.

How to select and adapt existing information to the needs of your communication
There may be different sources of the information you want to convey in different forms. You will need to be able to select the existing information that most closely matches the purpose of your communication and the needs of your audience.

You may not be able to find information that exactly matches your requirements. If that is so, you will need to adapt the information you find. This may involve simplifying the language used in a text article, cropping a photograph or adding an arrow to a map to indicate a location, for example. If you use or adapt existing information, it is important that you identify and credit its source.

When to create original information
Sometimes you will need to create your own original information. If you are producing a *curriculum vitae (cv)* and letter to apply for a job, the information you include in it will be original information about you.

> **Key term**
>
> *Curriculum vitae*: called a resume in the US, this is a document that includes your personal details and your education and employment history.

When to blend existing and original information
Often you will need to blend your own original information with existing information. For example, you may carry out a survey to find out how your fellow students spend their leisure time and present your results alongside national statistics obtained from existing sources.

How to maintain a consistent style throughout a communication
When you are creating a long document or presentation, it is important that it has a consistent style throughout. The use of named heading styles, templates and master page layouts will help you to achieve this. A master page layout allows you to set the layout that all the pages in a document or presentation will follow. This will include things like the background and text colours, the size of margins, the position of page numbers, the font style and size for titles and body text and the style of bullets. Slide presentations can be formatted in a similar way (see Figure 1.27).

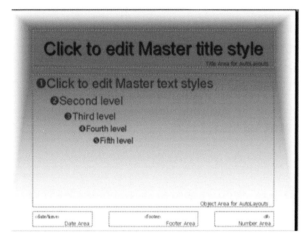

FIGURE 1.27 *Master slide*

How to combine text, sound, graphics, video and number information harmoniously
In a previous section we discussed the use of different types of media to improve presentation style. Often you will need to combine different types of information and media in a communication. It is very easy to combine different types of information badly. Too many graphics or video clips will compete with each other for the viewer's attention, reducing their effectiveness. When you are combining text and graphics you need to consider the position of each carefully, so that there is an overall balance to the document, and so that pictures are as near as possible to the passage of text they illustrate. Whichever types of information you are combining, you should try to achieve a

harmonious balance, so that each type of information is communicated effectively without undermining others.

How to evaluate the communications you produce

You will need to produce many different communications to refine your skills in presenting information and to evaluate each communication you produce so that future ones will be more effective. You will need to ask yourself and others a number of questions such as:

* is the style of language suitable for the purpose?

* is the style of language suitable for the intended audience?

* does the presentation style match the purpose of the communication?

* does the presentation style appeal to the intended audience?

* will the audience understand what I am trying to say?

* does the communication have the impact I wanted to achieve?

* how could I improve the communication to make it more effective?

Think it over...

In a group, discuss and evaluate some of the communications you have created. Use the questions just listed as the basis for your discussion.

How organisations present information

Every organisation is made up of a group of people who work together to make something or provide a service. You will learn more about what organisations are and how they operate in Unit 2: How organisations use ICT. In this chapter we will look specifically at why and how organisations present information, both within the organisation and outside it.

Why, and how, organisations present information both within, and outside, the organisation

All organisations need to communicate information. Internal communications may include memos and emails sent by managers to their staff, or from one member of staff to another. Large organisations may create multimedia presentations for training staff or informing them of developments within the organisation. The larger the organisation, the more internal communication will be needed to keep it running smoothly. Organisations also need to communicate with outsiders, including other organisations. External communications will be with customers, suppliers, official bodies such as the Inland Revenue and with the general public. Communication with customers may include letters, invoices, brochures and, increasingly, emails and websites. Organisations will send orders to suppliers and will have to send financial information to the Inland Revenue. There are many different ways that organisations communicate with the general public, including advertisements, posters and flyers. Some may even display visual presentations in public places to inform people about the organisation and its products or services.

Organisations present information externally through branding and advertising. This helps customer loyalty, gives quicker identification and reinforces the link between validity and reliability, therefore giving an impression of trust. The presentation of internal information gives branding for employees, consistency of standards, and saves time and money.

Typical uses of illustrations, technical drawings, pictures and artwork

Letters, invoices and similar documents will not include graphical information other than the company logo and possibly logos of other organisations, such as trade bodies, that they belong to. Other types of communication from organisations will include graphical information in different forms. A builder developing a new block of flats may produce publicity material that includes artists' impressions to illustrate what the finished block will look like (see Figure 1.28).

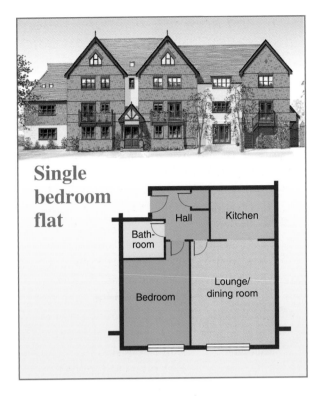

Single bedroom flat

Hall

Kitchen

Bath-room

Bedroom

Lounge/dining room

FIGURE 1.28 *An artist's impression*

each line of the address, for example. It is also usual for all the items in a letter to start at the left margin with paragraph breaks being shown by a blank line. Some letters are fully blocked, which means that the text of the letter is fully justified (see page 27). Where the organisation sending the letter is a company, the company's full name, registration number and the address of the registered office must appear on the letter (see Figure 1.29). The address may be different from that from which the letter is being sent and is often included in a smaller font size as a footer.

Harcourt Education Limited
Registered Office: Halley Court, Jordan Hill, Oxford OX2 8EJ

Registered in England: Number 3099304

FIGURE 1.29 *Section of Heinemann notepaper showing registered office details*

The material may also include technical drawings such as the floor plans of different flats. All of this graphical information will enable the builder to sell the flats before they have even been built. A company that makes and sells self-assembly furniture will provide instructions, including technical drawings, for assembling it. A school prospectus is likely to include photographs of staff, pupils and different features of the school. Most advertisements, publicity flyers, newsletters and similar documents, as well as visual and multimedia presentations will include pictures and artwork of one kind or another.

Commonly accepted standards for the layout of formal documents

There are commonly accepted standards for the layout of formal documents and certain items of information that must appear on them. We discussed the positioning of information on business letters in a previous section. Most business letters use a style called open punctuation. This means that the only punctuation used is in the body of the letter so that it makes sense: there are no commas after

Essential information that appears on formal documents

Other documents also have information that must be included for legal or other reasons. An invoice (see Figure 1.30) will include an invoice number for easy reference. It must show the address of the company sending the invoice so that the customer knows where to send payment. As with a letter, the company's registration details must also appear. The invoice will also include the terms under which payment must be made, for example within 30 days. If the company is VAT registered, their VAT registration number and the amount of VAT charged must appear on the invoice. The invoice will also include the customer's address and the delivery address if it is different.

A fax header sheet should indicate the number of pages being sent and the telephone number of the sender. The receiver then knows when all the pages have arrived and can contact the sender if there is a problem.

```
Walter's Widgets,
Unit 24,
Sprocket Industrial Estate,
Anyhampton,
Somewhereshire
SM1 2AB
                        INVOICE

Invoice No. INV1234567
Invoice Date: 1/8/05

Customer:
The Widget Shop,
123 Rubble Road,
Anyhampton,
Somewhereshire
SM1 2CD
```

Item	Quantity	Price per unit	Total
Round Widget	10	£3.50	£35.00
Square Widget	10	£4.50	£45.00
Curved Widget	20	£2.50	£50.00
		Sub Total	£130.00
		VAT @ 17.5%	£22.75
		GRAND TOTAL	**£152.75**

```
Payment Terms: 30 days

VAT No. 1234567890
```

FIGURE 1.30 *A sample invoice*

FIGURE 1.31 *Logos*

Methods of presenting a corporate image

Most organisations want to present a corporate image when they communicate externally. Indeed, some organisations spend very large sums of money designing and implementing a corporate image so that all their communications are instantly recognisable.

Part of an organisation's corporate image may be a logo (see Figure 1.31), but there will also be presentation rules, or house style, that all communications must follow. These rules may include the style, colour and size of fonts used for different documents, the size of margins, when and how the company logo is used, where it should be positioned, and so on. Some large organisations may provide their staff with a booklet or other document containing detailed instructions on how to create different communications in the house style.

How templates might be used to enforce corporate standards

Another way of ensuring that all communications conform to the organisation's house style is to provide staff with templates that they must use. These templates can be set up with the correct page layout and font styles so that staff simply need to click on them and enter the information.

Types of documents

Earlier in this chapter we looked at different writing and presentation styles. In this section we are going to consider these in relation to different types of communications used by organisations.

Publicity flyers

Publicity flyers (see Figure 1.32) may be handed out to people, posted through letterboxes or left in places such as reception areas or stations for people

FIGURE 1.32 *A flyer*

to pick up. They are usually printed on a single sheet of paper (usually A4 or A5) either on one or both sides, and, if A4, may be folded in half or into three. Publicity flyers need to grab people's attention. Presentation techniques such as large font sizes, colour and images will be used to do so. The writing style will often be informal, with short, easy-to-read statements rather than long sentences.

Questionnaires

Organisations use questionnaires for a variety of reasons. A common reason is to get feedback from customers on the quality of the goods or services the organisation provides. Organisations that provide a guarantee for the goods they sell often ask customers to register the product and complete a 'lifestyle' questionnaire (see Figure 1.33).

This allows the organisation to build a profile of the type of customers who buy its products. Whatever the purpose of the questionnaire, it is important that it is easy to understand and easy to complete. Instructions and questions must be

clear and easy to understand. Closed or limited response questions will probably be used with tick boxes for responses. A common method to obtain an opinion is to ask the respondent to indicate a number on a given scale or select a descriptor. For example, How would you rate the quality of our service? 1 Excellent, 2 Good, 3 Average, 4 Poor, 5 Unacceptable. Where this technique is used, the numbers and descriptors need to be used consistently. It is common to find a

A. YOUR NAME & ADDRESS

GUIDANCE NOTES
1. Please answer questions on behalf of yourself, your partner or your household as appropriate Of course, you can always discuss your answers with other members of your family.
2. Please feel free to ignore particular questions if you wish. Your remaining answers are still of value.
3. Please write in CAPITAL letters – tick boxes like this. ✔
4. If you make a mistake, simply cross it out and continue.
5. Some of the questions will relate to you or your partner. Please ask your partner before providing information on their behalf.

Your name: Mr ☐ Mrs ☐ Miss ☐ Ms ☐

Initials

Surname

Address

Town

County

Postcode

Telephone number:

Your mobile number:

e-mail address: @

Are you?
Married 01 ☐ Single 02 ☐ Divorced/Separated 03 ☐ Widowed 04 ☐ Living Together 05 ☐

If applicable, please write in the date you were married:

Your partner's name: Mr ☐ Mrs ☐ Miss ☐ Ms ☐

Initials

Surname

Your partner's mobile number:

Your partner's e-mail address: @

What are the dates of birth of: You   Your Partner

GENERAL INTERESTS

1. Please tick the leisure interests and activities which you and your partner enjoy regularly: *(Please tick all that apply)*

	You	Ptnr		You	Ptnr
Art	01 ☐	18 ☐	Football Pools	35 ☐	52 ☐
Arts & Crafts	02 ☐	19 ☐	Foreign Travel	36 ☐	53 ☐
Antiques	03 ☐	20 ☐	Gardening	37 ☐	54 ☐
Astrology/Horoscopes	04 ☐	21 ☐	Health Foods	38 ☐	55 ☐
Betting	05 ☐	22 ☐	Home Baking	39 ☐	56 ☐
Book Reading	06 ☐	23 ☐	Live Sports Events	40 ☐	57 ☐
Bingo	07 ☐	24 ☐	Motoring	41 ☐	58 ☐
Catalogue Shopping	08 ☐	25 ☐	Motorsports	42 ☐	59 ☐
Cigarette Smoking	09 ☐	26 ☐	National Lottery	43 ☐	60 ☐
Cinema	10 ☐	27 ☐	National Trust	44 ☐	61 ☐
Collectibles	11 ☐	28 ☐	Nightclubs	45 ☐	62 ☐
Computer Games	12 ☐	29 ☐	Personal Finance	46 ☐	63 ☐
Cookery	13 ☐	30 ☐	Science/Technology	47 ☐	64 ☐
Current Affairs	14 ☐	31 ☐	Slimming	48 ☐	65 ☐
D I Y	15 ☐	32 ☐	Theatre	49 ☐	66 ☐
Eating Out	16 ☐	33 ☐	Visiting Pubs	50 ☐	67 ☐
Fashion	17 ☐	34 ☐	Wildlife	51 ☐	68 ☐

2. Have you taken (in the last 3 years), or are you considering taking, any of the following types of holiday? *(Please tick all that apply)*

	Taken	May Take		Taken	May Take
Apartment/Self Catering	01 ☐	07 ☐	Motoring	13 ☐	19 ☐
Citybreak	02 ☐	08 ☐	Package Holiday	14 ☐	20 ☐
Coach Holiday	03 ☐	09 ☐	Skiing	15 ☐	21 ☐
Cruise	04 ☐	10 ☐	UK Short Break	16 ☐	22 ☐
Hotel UK	05 ☐	11 ☐	Walking/Trekking	17 ☐	23 ☐
Long Haul	06 ☐	12 ☐	Winter Sun	18 ☐	24 ☐

3. On average, how many weeks a year do you spend abroad?
One-two 01 ☐   Three-four 02 ☐   Five or more 03 ☐

FIGURE 1.33 *A lifestyle questionnaire*

number of such questions in a table format. Often, an even number of options is provided to prevent people simply choosing the middle one. Depending on the purpose of the questionnaire, there may also be lines for the respondent to write comments.

Business letters

We have already discussed many of the presentation styles and common standards used for business letters. The writing style used will depend on the reason the letter is being sent. Many organisations send out letters to existing and potential customers using mailing lists. These letters try to persuade people to buy the product or service the organisation offers. Such letters will often be written in a more informal style and using persuasive language. On the other hand, a letter to a customer in response to a complaint is likely to be written in a more formal style of language.

Newsletters

Newsletters may be internal to an organisation to keep its employees informed about what is happening in the organisation, for example the vocational department internal newsletter may make the organisation aware of the newly formed team; or it may be an external document for customers or the general public. There are few common standards for such documents, although most will use a fairly informal writing style. Most newsletters will have a title, even if it is just the name of the organisation such as 'Banks and Co Staff Newsletter'. A date or some indication of when it was issued, such as 'Spring 2005', is vital. Many newsletters will use columns and most will include at least some pictures. The size of the newsletter and the presentation techniques used will depend on a number of factors such as the size of the organisation and how often it is published. A large organisation that produces a quarterly newsletter for its staff may produce a high-quality, colour document of several pages, which includes a number of photographs and other graphics (see Figure 1.34). A small charity that produces a monthly newsletter for subscribers may produce a single-page black and white newsletter with few pictures so as to keep production costs to a minimum.

Visual presentations

Organisations use visual (or slide) presentations for two main purposes. One of these purposes is to accompany a talk to an audience; the other is as an unattended, automatic 'rolling' presentation in a reception area, airport or other public place. In either case, the amount of text on each slide should be kept to a minimum, using large font sizes that are easy to read from a distance. The text is often displayed as bullet points. Presentation techniques should be used consistently and colours chosen carefully. Most slide presentations include graphic images, including charts or graphs. The golden rule is only one graphic image per slide.

Brochures

Brochures come in all shapes and sizes and for a variety of purposes. Many brochures will advertise the goods or services that an organisation sells. It is, therefore, vital that the name of the organisation and its contact details are clearly displayed. Such brochures will almost always include photographs and other images. The text may be fairly informal and descriptive, trying to show the products or services in the best light. However, many brochures will include terms and conditions that will be written in a formal style to meet legal requirements.

Itineraries

An itinerary provides details of a trip that is going to happen. Travel agents and tour operators will provide itineraries for their customers; other organisations may provide itineraries for staff going on business trips. An itinerary will include

FIREPOWER
THE ROYAL ARTILLERY MUSEUM

CELEBRATIONS AS DAME VERA LYNN OPENS PHASE TWO OF FIREPOWER – by Brigadier Ken Timbers

Opening the two new galleries in Building 41 at the end of March was, for me, an occasion of mixed feelings. On the one hand, it was wonderful to have the opportunity at last to show off the big guns of the post-WW2 era, together with some of the splendid trophies from the Rotunda. On the other, it was a moment to reflect on the fact that we still have much of the RA Historical Trust's collection to bring into play, and little prospect of being able to show it until the funding situation improves.

The opening ceremony, performed so gracefully by Dame Vera Lynn, was very well attended by a large gathering of supporters of the Museum, including Mrs April Clavell and Major Tony Howitt, two of our major benefactors. Included among the guests were representatives of the firms which had done the work of developing the galleries. It is impossible in the space available here to name all those who had a hand in the project, but I would like to pick out the Project Manager, Peter Thompson of Slough Estates, the architects, Austin:Smith Lord and, in particular, their design team headed by Bob Aitken, and the main building contractors, Hillmans. The supporting team from the Museum, too, deserves a mention: Les Smith, Matthew Buck, Paul Evans and Marc Sherriff all played a significant part in bringing the project to a successful conclusion.

The Cold War gallery was produced on a shoestring. The grant from the European Regional Development Fund had to be directed primarily towards the preparation of the building, so there was little left with which to develop the gallery itself. With this in mind, it is amazing what can be done by a designer with flair, using modern museum techniques. The use of high screens to break up the space into manageable proportions, with huge poster images to provide contemporary images, proved to be a major contribution to the success of the gallery. Innovative lighting stands, display boards and audio handsets have added another interesting dimension, so that the collection of objects on display is given the best possible interpretation.

Dame Vera officially opens the Cold War Gallery

Smiles all round as Mitchell Mannion (aged 10) from Mulgrave Primary School, Woolwich presents Dame Vera with a beautiful basket of flowers.

There remains much to be done. One of the aspects which we would have liked to highlight—a large 'sand table' map display of an armoured division deployed in Germany during the Cold War—had to be shelved for lack of funds, but the concept has been fully developed and will be brought forward as soon as funding permits. Another feature to come in due course is the grouping of ammunition displays with the equipment exhibited: it was delayed at this point simply to ensure that the objects could be enclosed to protect them from careless handling—we can't afford to be sued by a visitor who topples a 155mm shell onto his foot!

Mrs Clavell unveiling the sign with the assistance of Regimental Colonel Simon Hutchinson

Naming of James Clavell Square

On the same day as the opening of the Cold War Gallery Dame Vera joined visitors to welcome Mrs April Clavell to officially open 'James Clavell Square'. This is the area immediately outside the Clavell Library and Archives.

The Regimental Colonel, Simon Hutchinson, warmly introduced Mrs Clavell as one of Firepower's loyal supporters. Mrs Clavell sponsored The Library and Archives in memory of her late husband, the author James Clavell and Colonel Hutchinson gave the audience gathered an insight into the author's works such as 'King Rat' and 'Shogun'.

Mrs Clavell said she was extremely proud to have his name associated with Firepower and the Royal Arsenal.

FIGURE 1.34 *A newsletter*

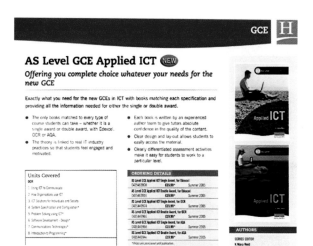

FIGURE 1.35 *Extract from Heinemann catalogue*

details of the date, time, departure and arrival point for each journey, along with dates and the location of any accommodation booked. These will usually be in the order they are to happen. For clarity, the information is often shown in a table (see Figure 1.36). It is vital that the information on an itinerary is accurate. If not, people may miss trains or flights, or go to the wrong hotel.

Forms to collect information from people

Questionnaires are one way that organisations collect information from people, but they are not the only way. You have probably filled in application forms for all sorts of reasons, for example to apply for your college or a job, to get a passport or a driving licence or to become a member of a club.

The layout of such forms is very important. It must be clear where the person filling it in should write their information and there must be enough space for them to do so. Boxes and tables are often used for this. There are many poorly designed forms that do not provide sufficient space for responses. The language used needs to be clear so that the reader knows what information they must provide. Passport application forms, for example, come with a separate instruction booklet to help you complete them correctly. Many government agencies use forms to collect information from people. For example, each year

many people have to complete a Tax Return for the Inland Revenue, and once every ten years every household in the country must complete a census form.

Think it over...

Why do government agencies often ask you to write in ink and capital letters?

Business reports

Business reports are usually fairly long formal documents. They may be written to summarise some research findings or they may be a report on the year's activities for shareholders and others. Reports will probably start with an introduction or an abstract. An abstract is a summary of what is included in the report so that people can get an overview without having to read the whole report. The report will be divided up into sections with headings and often numbered paragraphs. It will end with a conclusion or some closing remarks. Most reports will include a list of contents and an alphabetical index. There may also be a number of appendices. Reports may include photographs, other pictures and graphs or charts, as well as tables of figures. Some end-of-year reports issued by large organisations are very glossy high-quality documents.

Technical specifications

Manufacturing organisations produce technical specifications (see Figure 1.38) to give precise technical information about their products. They will use clear technical language and numerical information. This may be presented in tables for ease of reading. Technical drawings may also be included.

Web pages

Most organisations have their own website, as many people will search the WWW for what they require (see Figure 1.39). It is very important that the web pages are well designed, easy to navigate and provide the information people need.

Itinerary for forthcoming visits to Regional Offices

The following meetings have been organised for the week beginning 22/06/05.

Day	Regional Office	Start time
Monday	Midlands Region, Birmingham	10.30
Tuesday	North Region, Leeds	10.00
Wednesday	Scotland and Islands Region, Edinburgh	11.00
Thursday	North and Borders Region, Newcastle	10.00
Friday	Central Region, Manchester	11.00

Travel and overnight accommodation details are shown below. You may use taxis to travel from the train station to the regional office and from the regional office to your hotel – don't forget to get receipts. Location maps are attached.

Date	Depart	Arrive	Hotel
22/06/05	London Marylebone Time: 0715	Birmingham Snow Hill Time: 0943	Holiday Inn, Great Barr
23/06/05	Birmingham New Street Time: 0703	Leeds Central Time: 0905	Holiday Inn, City Centre
24/06/05	Leeds Central Time: 0710	Edinburgh Waverley Time: 1018	Holiday Inn, City Centre
25/06/05	Edinburgh Waverley Time: 0807	Newcastle Central Time: 0939	Holiday Inn, Washington Tyne & Wear
26/06/05	Newcastle Central Time: 0726	Manchester Picadilly Time: 1026	Crowne Plaza, Manchester Airport
26/06/05	Manchester Picadilly Time: 1820	London Euston Time: 2110	

FIGURE 1.36 *An itinerary*

Poorly designed web pages will reflect badly on the organisation. If people can't move around the site easily and find what they are looking for, they will become frustrated and look elsewhere. Also, whilst high levels of graphics and other multimedia features may seem appealing, not everyone has fast access to the Internet.

Multimedia presentations

Organisations may use multimedia presentations internally for training staff or for annual reports on how well the company has done and to outline future strategy. Multimedia presentations are also used externally for promoting products and services, for example at trade fairs. High-quality multimedia presentations are expensive

> **✱ REMEMBER!**
>
> ✱ Organisations communicate internally with members of their staff and externally with customers, suppliers, the general public and other organisations.
>
> ✱ Many organisations adopt a house style for all external communications, to present a corporate image.
>
> ✱ As you have learnt throughout this chapter, the writing and presentation styles used in business communications are dependent on the purpose, audience and communication method and must be appropriate to these.
>
> ✱ There are common standards for the layout of many business documents.

Specifications

Product type	: Digital camera (for shooting and displaying)
Recording system	
Still picture	: Digital recording, JPEG (in accordance with Design rule for Camera File system (DCF)), Exif 2.2, Digital Print Order Format (DPOF), PRINT Image Matching II
Movie	: QuickTime Motion JPEG support
Memory	: xD-Picture Card (16 – 256MB)

No. of storable pictures (when a 16 MB Card is used) :

Resolution	Record mode/ No. of storable pictures			
	Model A		Model B	
2272 × 1704	SHQ	5	—	—
	HQ	16		
2048 × 1536	SQ1	20	SHQ	6
			HQ	20
1600 × 1200	SQ2	24	SQ1	24
1280 × 960		38		38
1024 × 768		58	SQ2	58
640 × 480		99		99

Record mode	Resolution (Frames/sec)	Memory capacity in sec. per movie
HQ	320 × 240 (15 frames/sec)	16
SQ	160 × 120 (15 frames/sec)	70

No. of effective pixels

MODEL A	: 3,200,000 pixels
MODEL B	: 4,000,000 pixels

FIGURE 1.38 *Part of the technical specification for a digital camera*

to produce but relatively cheap to copy and distribute. For this reason, it is likely to be only large organisations who communicate in this way.

Knowledge check

1 How can templates be used to enforce a corporate style?

2 What features would you expect a publicity flyer to include?

3 How will a visual presentation best meet the needs of its audience?

4 What design features are important for an organisation's website?

Standard ways of working

While you are carrying out your work for the GCE in Applied ICT, you will need to follow standard ways of working. Organisations in which you will work also have similar rules and guidelines to ensure the security of their data, safety of staff and the effectiveness of the workforce.

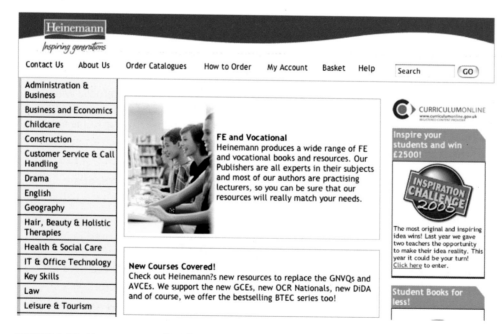

FIGURE 1.39 *Home page of Heinemann website*

Why these are important to ICT

Information that is held on computer systems can be easily lost or misused. Much of the information stored will be confidential, either personal information about individuals or information about the organisation that other people could use against it. Without standard ways of working, unauthorised persons may gain access to this confidential information. It is very easy to copy data that is held in computer files. Without standard ways of working, people could copy others' original work and present it as their own. Data files held on computer systems can be easily lost or corrupted, for example by viruses or hardware failure. If a computer system is physically damaged, it may not be possible to recover the data held on it. Also, the use of computers makes it very easy to present information in a professional way. Information that is presented professionally is likely to be believed, even if it is not accurate.

Managing your work

While you are working towards this qualification, you will have a number of assignments to complete and limited time to complete them in. When you are given an assignment, you will also be told when you must hand it in. You will need to look carefully at what you are being asked to do, decide how long each task will take you and then plan when and how you will complete each task so that you can produce everything by the deadline. If you do not plan your work you will be rushing to complete it and will produce work of poor quality. *The ability to plan work to meet deadlines is an important skill that you will find useful in the future.*

This unit is about presenting information. One aspect of managing your work is to make correct use of facilities such as spaces, tabs and indents to lay out your work consistently. This will also make editing easier.

How often have you wanted to reopen a file and not been able to remember where you stored it (see Figure 1.40) or what you called it?

An important aspect of managing your work is to use filenames that are sensible and that remind

FIGURE 1.40 *'I know I saved that file somewhere!'*

you of what the file contains. Most modern software allows you to use long filenames, making it easy to give files meaningful names. How you organise your file storage and where you store files is equally important. If you set up folders with meaningful names and make sure that you always store files in the appropriate folder, you will always be able to find the file you are looking for.

Computers and other ICT equipment do not always work as they should. It can be very frustrating and prevent you getting on with your work if problems occur. Many problems happen more than once and can be solved relatively easily providing you can remember what to do. Keeping a log of any problems that occur and how you solved them will ensure that you can solve similar problems in the future (see Table 1.4).

Keeping information secure

Information needs to be protected from, for example, theft, loss, viruses and fire. Physical security such as locks on doors and bars on windows is one way to protect information from theft. However, it is not always necessary to be in

DATE	PROBLEM	SOLUTION

TABLE 1.4 *Problem log*

the same room or even the same building as the computer storing the information to steal it. For this reason, so called logical security is also needed. This includes the use of passwords and access rights, so that only authorised people can access the information. To maintain security it is important that passwords are kept secret. You should also choose passwords that are not easy to guess – a random selection of letters and numbers is best. You should change passwords regularly and always if you think someone else knows it.

One reason for keeping information secure from theft and unauthorised access is confidentiality. Confidential information is information that individuals or organisations do not want others to know. Medical, criminal and financial records should all be kept confidential. As well as keeping such information secure, the people who work with confidential information must not pass it on to others.

Viruses are computer programs that replicate themselves and spread from computer to computer, either via removable storage media such as floppy disks, or via networks, especially the Internet.

Think it over...

How many viruses have you encountered or know of? Research the WWW for information.

Although not all viruses are malicious, most are, causing the files on infected computers to become corrupted, or allowing the writer of the virus to access the files on the infected system. The main protection against viruses is to install and use virus checking software. However, as new viruses are being developed all the time, this will be effective only if the software is regularly updated. Restricting the use of the Internet and of removable storage media can also provide some protection against viruses.

The main way of protecting information stored on a computer system from loss is to keep a backup. This is a second copy of the information that can be used if the original is lost. To be of value, backups need to be taken frequently and dated so that you know when each was saved. Backups also need to be stored in a different location from the original information. To protect against fire, the backup should be kept in a fireproof safe, or preferably in a different building. If the original information is lost, the most recent backup can be used to restore the information. However, it will not be possible to restore any information that has been created since the backup was taken.

Theory into practice

Find out what your college/organisation does about backups.

Another way of protecting information from loss is to save your work regularly using different filenames. This is particularly important before you make significant changes. If, by making the changes, you lose the information, you can always go back to the previous version.

One of the reasons why standard ways of working are important is to stop people copying original work and presenting it as their own. Computer programs, words, pictures, graphic images and music that have been created by other people are protected by copyright. The person who created or owns the material has the copyright to it. The Copyright, Designs and Patents Act (1980) determines how others can use the material. You will learn more about this Act in Unit 2: How organisations use ICT. In general, you must not use the work of others without their permission (see Figure 1.41 for a sample letter requesting permission). Where you do use the work of others, you must acknowledge the source, either with a suitable reference, or by including it in your bibliography.

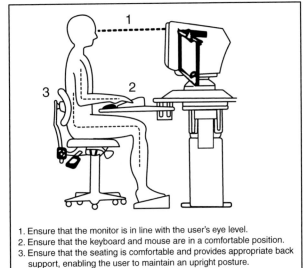

1. Ensure that the monitor is in line with the user's eye level.
2. Ensure that the keyboard and mouse are in a comfortable position.
3. Ensure that the seating is comfortable and provides appropriate back support, enabling the user to maintain an upright posture.

FIGURE 1.42 *Safe-sitting position*

Heinemann

Halley Court
Jordan Hill
Oxford OX2 8EJ

Tel: +44 (0)1865 311366
Fax: +44 (0)1865 314140
Web: www.heinemann.co.uk

Dear XX,

I am writing to request permission to use XXX in our forthcoming educational publication, *XXX*.

The details of the forthcoming publication are as follows:

Title: *XXX*
Author: XX
Extent: XX
Price: XX
Pub. date: XX

The rights we are seeking are world rights in all languages for reproduction in all forms and media, including electronic media, in this and any future revisions and editions of the book published by [imprint] and under licence from [imprint], and for publication in promotional material for the book. Should you not control these rights in their entirety, would you kindly let me know to whom I must write.

The deadline for this project is XX and I would be grateful if you could let me know at your earliest convenience whether you can grant us permission to use this material and, if so, what fee and form of acknowledgement you might require.

For your convenience a release form is provided below and a copy of this letter is enclosed for your files.

Yours sincerely,

XX

Permission is hereby granted to reproduce the material requested above on the terms set out in this letter for a fee of _____.

Acknowledgement: _____

Signed: _____ Date: _____

FIGURE 1.41 *A sample letter for permission*

Working safely

Although the ICT working environment is fairly safe, there are some health and safety issues that you need to be aware of. Health issues tend to relate to bad posture, physical stress and eyestrain, while safety issues relate to hazards resulting from equipment or workplace layout.

An important part of reducing problems caused by poor posture and physical stress is comfortable seating. Chairs should be adjustable and provide good support for your back. A comfortable chair alone will not prevent these problems. You must make sure that the desk, VDU and keyboard are positioned correctly and your chair is correctly adjusted. Ideally, your eyes should be level with or slightly above the top of the monitor, your wrists should be straight with your forearms parallel with the floor and your feet should be flat on the floor with your thighs also parallel to it (see Figure 1.42).

However comfortable and well positioned your workstation is, you should try to take brief rest periods at regular intervals. In particular, you should avoid long periods of continuous VDU work. Try to organise your work so that periods spent at the computer are broken up with other activities. When you take a break from work, get up and walk around, rather than play a computer game. As well as taking breaks, to help prevent eyestrain, you should exercise the muscles in your eyes by focusing on near and distant objects every so often. It is, therefore, important that the computer's surroundings provide the opportunity for you to do this.

The two main safety issues in an ICT environment are tripping and electrical hazards. Tripping hazards can be prevented by careful layout of cables and equipment. Cables should not cross walkways and should be enclosed in trunking. To prevent electrical hazards, sufficient electrical sockets should be available to prevent overloading, and all electrical cables should be properly insulated.

> **✳ REMEMBER!**
>
> Standard ways of working are designed to ensure that:
>
> ✳ work is carried out efficiently – by planning, using techniques to ensure consistent layout, using meaningful filenames and storing files in a directory/folder structure and by keeping a log of problems
>
> ✳ information is kept secure – by using physical security and passwords, checking for viruses, protecting confidentiality, respecting copyright, keeping backups and saving regularly with different filenames
>
> ✳ work is carried out safely – by adjusting your workstation and maintaining good posture, taking regular breaks, focusing on near and distant objects, reducing trip hazards such as trailing cables, and ensuring electrical safety.

Knowledge check

1 Give five reasons why standard ways of working are important.

2 How can you ensure that, in the future, you will be able to find files that you save?

3 What types of information are confidential and why should confidentiality be protected?

4 How can you ensure that information is not lost if a fire destroys your computer?

5 What health and safety hazards are associated with the ICT working environment and how can they be avoided?

Assessment evidence

A new independent travel agent is opening in a town near where you live. They will specialise in organising activity holidays in the UK and overseas. They have asked you to help them create the communications they need to advertise and run the business.

Task 1

Collect two types of documents from each of three organisations. Ideally, these documents should be from three different travel agents. It should be relatively easy to collect brochures, and most travel agents will also have a website. Most brochures will also include a booking form. You may be able to get hold of letters from the travel agents or travel itineraries, but remember you must collect the same two types of document from all three travel agents.

Study the documents carefully and write a report describing and comparing them. You will need to answer some or all of these questions when you are writing your report.

✳ What is the specific purpose of each document?

✳ What layout has been used for each document?

✳ What are the good points, if any, of each document's presentation?

✳ What are the bad points, if any, of each document's presentation?

✳ What comparisons can be made between the presentation styles of similar documents?

✳ What are the good points, if any, of each document's writing style?

✳ What are the bad points, if any, of each document's writing style?

✳ What comparisons can be made between the writing styles of similar documents?

✳ Has a house style been used for the two documents from the same organisation?

✳ How is this house style demonstrated?

✳ How well does each document meet its purpose?

✳ Are there any improvements that could be made to each document? What are they?

As a minimum you must describe the layout and/or the purpose of each document and identify some good and bad points about the writing and/or presentation styles of similar documents. To reach the second mark band, you must describe both the layout and purpose of each document and identify good and bad points about both the writing and presentation styles of similar items. You must also make some comment on their suitability for purpose, their use of house style and/or how they could be improved. Your report must contain few spelling, punctuation and grammar errors. To reach the highest mark band, your descriptions of the layout and purpose of the documents must be detailed and you must accurately identify good and bad points about writing and presentation styles of similar items. You must comment on the suitability for purpose, use of house style and how the documents could be improved. Your report must be consistently well structured and contain few, if any, errors in spelling, punctuation and grammar. If you provide detailed answers to all of the questions and take care over your use of English when writing your report, you should be able to reach this mark band.

Tasks 2–7

When you are carrying out the remaining tasks you should:

✳ plan the content and layout of each communication – if you produce little evidence of planning, you will reach only the lowest mark band; outline plans will gain the second mark band and detailed plans will enable you to reach the highest mark band

✳ include a list of any information sources you use – a simple list of sources is the minimum requirement; to reach the second mark band this will need to be organised in an appropriate way, and for the highest mark band you must produce a detailed bibliography

✳ create new information and locate, use and adapt existing information – as a minimum you should create new information that is clear, easy to understand and that uses a suitable style; to reach the second mark band you should locate, use and adapt existing information and combine it with information

you have created; to reach the highest mark band you must locate, adapt and combine information to create coherent easy-to-read communications of near-professional standard

✳ use common standards for layout where appropriate, for example use the standard layout for a business letter – you must do this to reach even the lowest mark band

✳ use different text styles, page layout and paragraph formatting to suit the purpose of a communication and improve its impact – to reach mark band one, these must suit the purpose of each communication; to achieve higher mark bands, they must also improve the impact of each communication

✳ combine different types of data – text, graphics (photographs, clipart, line drawings, graphs, charts), tables, borders, shading, sound, video clips – to suit the purpose of a communication and improve its impact – as a minimum you must combine two of these to suit the purpose of the communication; to reach the higher mark bands you will need to combine a range of types of data to also improve the impact of each communication

✳ use software to automate aspects of your communications, such as creating templates for standard layouts – this will contribute to the highest mark band

✳ include labelled and annotated draft copies of each communication to show how you developed them – if your annotations show how you placed information in appropriate positions and ensured correct and meaningful content, this will contribute to mark band two; for the highest mark band your annotations need to show how you achieved a consistent style and made good use of standard formats to organise a variety of different types of information in a coherent and easy-to-read way

✳ spell check and proof-read the content and layout and correct any errors found – at the lowest level you will show you can check the accuracy of the layout and content of your work and proof-read it, so few obvious errors remain; for higher mark bands your annotations will demonstrate how you checked your work carefully

* include a labelled final version of each communication

* evaluate each communication – as a minimum you must comment on how effective each communication is and suggest improvements; to reach the second band you also need to identify good and not so good features of each communication; to reach the highest mark band you must have identified strengths and weaknesses in your initial drafts and show how you refined them to meet the purpose more closely

* evaluate your performance in completing each task – as a minimum you must comment on how you went about carrying out the tasks; to reach the second mark band you will need to analyse how you carried out the tasks so that you could do it better next time; to reach the highest mark band you must also suggest how you might approach a similar task in the future.

To evaluate each communication you need to consider:

* what worked well – what is good about it

* what did not work – what is not so good

* how well it meets its purpose

* what you could improve if you created it again

* how you refined your drafts to meet the purpose more closely.

To evaluate your own performance you need to consider:

* what went well

* what went badly

* what you would do differently if you had to carry out a similar task in the future.

Task 2

The director of the travel agent wants to know about how information is communicated. Produce a presentation for the director of the travel agent on how information is communicated and the technologies that support

these communication methods. You may use presentation software to create an on-screen slide presentation with presenter notes to add detail or you may present the information in some other way.

As a minimum, you must briefly describe some of the methods used to communicate information and the technologies that support them. You will find information to help you earlier in this chapter but you must make sure that the information you include in your presentation is in your own words. To reach the second mark band, you must describe most of the methods used to communicate information and the technologies that support them. Your descriptions need to include some detail. To reach the highest mark band you need to provide detailed descriptions. At this level, you will need to supplement the information provided in this chapter with some research of your own.

Task 3

Create a letterhead for the tourist office and use it to produce a standard letter to a potential holidaymaker, outlining the type of holidays available, to be included with a copy of the brochure. Remember to use the standard layout for a business letter. You may also want to create a template so that similar letters can be more easily produced in future.

Task 4

Create a promotional flyer for an activity holiday in the UK – the location and activity is up to you. This is an opportunity to include suitable images as well as text.

Task 5

Create a website for the travel agent or a multimedia presentation that can be displayed in the travel agent's office. This is another opportunity to incorporate different types of data but if you are creating a website, do consider download times for those using dial-up services.

Task 6

Create some sample pages for a brochure detailing the holidays available. If you did not create a website in Task 5, these could be pages for an on-line brochure.

Task 7

Create a booking form to collect holidaymakers' details and the details of the holiday they want to book. Think carefully about the information you need to collect and the space needed for the information. The booking form can be paper-based or on-line.

Signposting for portfolio evidence

Currently, all of your evidence must be produced on paper. If you have created screen-based communications, you will need to provide screen prints or printouts to evidence your work. You will need to annotate these to indicate any features, such as sound, video or animation that are not obvious from the printouts. You should get your teacher to witness these features and initial or sign the printouts to confirm that the features work. For example, printing out a slide presentation as an audience handout with three slides to a page will provide space for you to add any necessary annotations.

You need to organise your work carefully. Make sure each piece of work is clearly labelled to show what it is and that your name is on each page. In particular, make sure that the draft and final copies of each communication are clearly labelled as such.

For Task 1, make sure you include copies of the documents you have compared. Your assessor and the moderator will not know whether you have described them accurately or not if you do not include them. For Tasks 2 to 7, put the work for each task in a logical order. A sensible order would be: plan, draft 1, draft 2 etc., final copy, evaluation. When you have put all your work in a sensible order, number all the pages and create a contents page to show where each piece of work is located.

UNIT 2

How organisations use ICT

Introduction

In this unit you will study organisations in detail. You will learn about how organisations are structured and how they use and exchange information. You will then consider how well ICT helps organisations and how it supports the different activities they undertake. Developments in ICT are offering organisations new opportunities in the ways they work and the way goods are produced. You will learn about some of these new opportunities. You will also learn about *legislation* relating to the use of ICT and the effect it has on organisations.

> **Key term**
>
> *Legislation*: laws or Acts of Parliament that must be obeyed.

How you will be assessed

This unit is assessed by an external assessment, the mark for which will be for the whole unit. You will need to be able to apply what you learn in this unit to an organisation described in a case study. You will have to carry out tasks related to this organisation and answer questions about it, as well as more general questions, in the examination.

What you need to learn

By studying this unit you will:

✳ know about the different types of organisation

* learn about the different *job functions* that appear within organisations. You will need to be able to describe these functions and the tasks that make up each particular one

* be able to interpret diagrams that show organisations' structures

* understand how organisations use information, including how it is collected, communicated and processed

* be able to describe the key systems used by large organisations

* be able to draw diagrams to describe the movement of information in organisations

* be able to describe the ICT systems used by organisations to support their operations, how the ICT systems support these operations and how they interact

* understand the impact that technological developments have had on *working practices*, including changes in working styles and employment opportunities and the possible effects on *employees*. You will need to be able to evaluate these effects on a particular organisation

* recognise how the introduction of *robotics* and other linked ICT systems have affected methods of production. You will need to be able to evaluate how a particular organisation has been affected

* understand the purpose of legislation related to using ICT, how organisations are affected by it and what, if anything, they must do to comply with the legislation.

Key terms

Job functions: staff who are responsible for carrying out specific tasks within an organisation, such as sales or finance.
Working practices: the way that work is organised and carried out.
Employees: the people who work for and are employed by an organisation.
Robotics: computer-controlled devices that are able to carry out tasks that would have previously been done by people.

Types of organisation

Organisations are made up of groups of people who use their own skills and other resources to make a product or provide a service. There are many different types of organisations of many different sizes. At the top of the range are the large multinational commercial companies, many of which are household names all over the world. Examples include oil companies such as Shell and BP; Coca Cola; sportswear companies such as Nike; electrical goods companies such as Sony; software companies such as Microsoft and many, many others.

Banks are organisations that provide financial services, and shops provide retail services. These range from large chains, such as Marks and Spencer or B&Q to small, privately owned corner shops. Other organisations provide utilities such as water, electricity and gas, or transport, including

CASE STUDY 1: FRANCEFILEZ

Introduction

Francefilez is a UK-based company that produces brochures advertising holiday homes in France and Spain. They produce a total of eight brochures, six for France and two for Spain, and each brochure is printed twice a year. All the brochures are distributed to newsagents and travel agencies throughout the UK. The company was founded in 1998 to produce a single brochure for holiday homes in France. This grew to the current six brochures by 2001, and the two Spanish brochures were launched in 2002.

The brochures are funded primarily by the advertisements placed by the owners of the holiday homes, but a number of airline and cross-channel travel companies have recently started to advertise in the brochures as well.

The company employs a total of 90 staff in two offices in Shropshire. The Head Office houses the finance and administration, sales and marketing, ICT services and human resources (HR) departments. The second office accommodates only the design and production department.

CASE STUDY 2: SOURCE COMPUTERS UK

Introduction

Source Computers UK is a wholesaler of computer components and software based in Essex. They supply computer equipment to a large number of local companies, computer shops and system builders in the area. They also sell to individuals who visit their premises. As well as selling computer components, Source Computers UK also use the components to build complete computer systems. They build and sell a small selection of standard systems, but will also build bespoke systems to meet customers' specific requirements.

Source Computers UK is a small business with fewer than 20 staff, based in a small unit in a business park. They keep the majority of components on site, but the main stock of more bulky components, such as monitors and computer cases, is kept in a secure lock-up some two miles away. The managing director, Mick, established the company in 2003, but all of the staff had previously worked together in other computer companies.

buses, trains and planes. All of these organisations aim to make a profit for their owners or shareholders.

Most hospitals, schools and colleges are examples of public-service organisations. Public-service organisations are funded by central or local government, through taxes, to provide health, education or other services to the public.

Before you learn about how ICT can help and support organisations, you will need to know how they are structured, their information needs, and describe the movement of information internally and externally within them.

In this unit we will consider two organisations: Francefilez and Source Computers UK. In the assessment for this unit, you will be provided with a similar case study about an organisation and be required to carry out tasks and answer questions based on that case study. However, you will also need to gain experience of real organisations either by visiting them, through work experience or a part-time job, or by people from the organisations coming to talk to you. You will gain more from your contacts with real organisations by having studied this unit, as it will help you to know what to look for and what questions to ask.

Functions within organisations

Within most organisations, there will be staff who are responsible for carrying out particular tasks. These tasks and responsibilities are known as job functions. In small organisations, one person may be responsible for more than one job function. Large organisations will have a *department* for each function. We will consider how organisations are structured later in this unit. In the following sections we will look at the different job functions that appear in many organisations, the tasks that make up those job functions and the other functions, organisations and people they communicate with.

> ### Key term
>
> *Department*: a group of people performing a particular job function under the direction of a department manager.

Accounts or finance

The accounts or finance job function in an organisation carries out all tasks relating to the money that comes into the organisation and the money that it pays out. This will include recording payments received for goods or services provided by the organisation and banking any payments made using cash or cheques. This function will arrange payment to suppliers for stock, raw materials or services, including water, gas, electricity and telephone, and rent or mortgage repayments for premises, as well as payments for loans. Many of these payments will be made by *BACS* transfer. Another important role of this job function is to arrange payment of staff wages. This too will probably done through BACS. Careful records must be kept of all financial transactions. The Inland Revenue will require accurate accounts so that the correct amount of tax can be collected, both from the organisation and from employees. Customs and Excise will require details of all transactions involving VAT (Value Added Tax). This will involve deducting the amount of VAT paid by the organisation to suppliers from the amount of VAT received by the organisation from customers, to find the amount of VAT the organisation must pay to Customs and Excise. Shareholders will also want accurate financial records as will the bank if the organisation needs to borrow money. As well

CASE STUDY 2: SOURCE COMPUTERS UK

Finance function

A finance administrator, Jane, and her assistant Mary, control the finance function in Source Computers. Between them they manage all aspects of purchasing, sales order processing and invoicing. All of these functions are computerised using an integrated finance package.

The purchasing manager, Dick, is primarily responsible for making regular purchases. Often he will do this by making telephone calls to the company's suppliers. He will then email the finance function details of the supplies purchased. The sales function can also make purchases, as often they have to ensure the availability of components for urgent orders. Sales also email details of the purchases to the finance function, with a copy sent to Dick. Jane or Mary then raises a confirmation purchase order (see Figure 2.1) that is sometimes posted but often emailed to the supplier. When an invoice is received from the supplier, it is Jane's responsibility to ensure that the supplier is paid.

The sales staff also email details of all customer orders to the finance function. Jane or Mary raises invoices for these orders and email or post them to the customers. They keep track of the payments received and send reminders if payments are overdue.

Mary is responsible for staff wages, which are paid monthly. Every month she sends a fax to the bureau company that runs their payroll. This fax either confirms that the information used to calculate the wages is unchanged, or it details any changes to the information, such as any paid overtime that staff have worked. Staff wages are paid directly into each individual member of staff's bank account by BACS transfer.

Purchase Order

Source Computers UK

78 Main Road

Billericay

Essex

SO11 2QQ

PO No: 226/3/117
Date: 20/03/06

Delivery Date: 20/03/06

Supplier
Screens UK
Radley House
Lower Marsh Street
Reading
RG1 3AZ

Qty	Item	Description	Discount %	Unit Price	Total
20	06392/15B	15 inch TFT Monitor Black	10	82.50	1500.00
15	06392/15s	15 inch TFT Monitor Silver		82.50	1237.50

Subtotal	2737.50
VAT	479.06
Bal Due	3216.56

FIGURE 2.1 *Example of a confirmation purchase order*

as communicating with these external organisations, this function will communicate information internally with most other functions, including sales, marketing and human resources.

Key term

BACS: Banks Automated Clearing System – a system that transfers money electronically from one bank account to another.

Purchasing

As we have already said, part of the role of the accounts or finance function is to pay for goods and services from suppliers. This is sometimes handled by a purchasing function that is purely responsible for the ordering of and payment for these goods and services. The purchasing function will raise *purchase orders* and receive and arrange payment of suppliers' invoices. Most other functions will communicate with purchasing when they need supplies of one kind or another.

Purchase orders: documents that list the goods or services that an organisation wants to purchase from a supplier – they are usually a two-part document: the top copy is sent to the supplier and the second copy is retained as a record of what has been ordered.

Sales order processing

Another section within the accounts or finance section is sales order processing. This is responsible for the administration of the organisation's financial dealing with customers. As part of this, it will organise contracts for services, receive sales orders, create and send invoices and receive and process customers' payments. There are close links between this function and the sales function.

Describe four essential tasks that make up the finance function of Source Computers UK.

Describe the links between the finance, purchasing and sales functions in Source Computers UK.

– accounts or finance function

Find out who is responsible for the accounts or finance function in your school or college. Interview them to find out how the tasks carried out are similar to or different from those in a *commercial organisation*.

Commercial organisation: an organisation that sells products or services in order to make a profit.

Sales

The sales function, as its name suggests, is responsible for selling an organisation's products or services to its customers. The tasks that are carried out by this job function will vary widely, depending on the nature of the organisation. In a shop, sales staff will help customers to find the products they require, take the customers' payments and wrap the purchases. They will also be responsible for ensuring there are goods on display and possibly taking orders for out-of-stock items. In a newspaper publishing organisation, the sales function will be responsible for selling advertising space in the newspapers. This is likely to involve *telesales*. Staff will take the customers' details and the details of the advertisements. These will be input into a computer system. The staff will then either take and check credit card details in payment or add the cost to an account so that the customer can be invoiced. A salesperson in a kitchen design company, for example, may visit each customer's home to discuss his or her requirements and to measure and design the kitchen. He or she will then produce a *quotation* for the customer. If the customer decides to accept the quotation, the salesperson will create an order for the parts and labour needed to complete the kitchen and will take a deposit from the customer. The sales function will communicate closely with marketing and accounts but will also communicate with other functions such as production and distribution.

Telesales: selling goods or services by taking orders over the telephone. It can also involve calling potential customers to try to get them to buy the product or service.
Quotation: details of what a product or service will cost.

Distribution

The distribution function is most likely to be found in organisations that make or sell goods, rather than those that provide a service. It is also

CASE STUDY 1: FRANCEFILEZ

Sales function

The sales function in Francefilez is part of the Sales and Marketing department. There are two sales managers in the department, one for France and one for Spain, both of whom report to the sales and marketing director. The sales function is organised into four teams, each with responsibility for selling advertising space in two brochures. Each team has a sales team leader. The sales teams vary in size, the largest having eight members and the smallest five members. Each sales assistant has responsibility for maintaining contact with a number of established customers, but they must also try to sell to a target number of new customers. Staff are paid a commission on sales. The main contact with customers is via the telephone, although FAX and email are increasingly used for confirmations, etc.

The sales teams have the support of an on-line database, which contains details of all existing customers, their sales history, any relevant notes and an interactive reminder system. The database also holds lists of potential customers. At the beginning of each day, sales staff log on to the system, check their own reminders and then start telephoning customers. All of them have been trained by the company in telesales techniques, and they normally follow a 'script' in their conversations. When a customer confirms that they want to place an advertisement, the sales assistant logs on to the sales order processing system to input the customer and advertisement details, method of payment, etc. As soon as this is completed the order is automatically directed to the administration department for further processing. The sales assistant will only need to be re-involved if any queries have to be taken up with the customer by telephone.

The sales team leaders are responsible only for the day-to-day management of their team members, helping with any queries that they might have and assisting with more difficult customer problems. The two sales managers, in addition to the day-to-day management of their sales teams, are also responsible for selling advertising space to selected airline and cross-channel operators. Because the revenue from such advertising has become increasingly important, most of the contact with these companies is conducted face to face.

sometimes called logistics. This function is responsible for moving goods from the factory, farm or other source to warehouses and then on to shops or directly to customers. This may involve sending goods by mail or using couriers. In this case, the distribution function will need to ensure that packages are correctly addressed and then either contact the postal or courier service to arrange a collection, or apply the correct postage and take them to the post office. Where goods are moved in bulk, such as from the factory to warehouses, they may be sent by rail or air freight or using road hauliers. The distribution function will be responsible for booking these services. Some organisations will have their own fleet of vans or trucks to deliver goods. For example, large supermarket chains have fleets of lorries to distribute goods from central warehouses to their stores.

Think it over...

It is likely that some of your group have part-time jobs in shops, supermarkets or elsewhere. Discuss the tasks that they and their work colleagues carry out as part of the sales function. Are there common tasks that are carried out in different types of shops? Are there any tasks that are unique to one organisation?

Knowledge check

The sales function in Francefilez uses telesales to sell space in their brochures. What does this involve?

What are the responsibilities of the sales team leaders and sales managers in Francefilez?

Distribution

Source Computers deliver about 60 per cent of their orders using a national courier service, who collect from their premises at 5.30pm Monday to Friday. The purchasing manager, Dick, is responsible for ensuring that all orders are picked, packed and ready for collection at this time. Only orders received before 4.00pm are guaranteed for despatch the same day.

The sales order processing system automatically produces despatch notes for orders that require delivery. Two copies are sent for printing at Dick's workstation. He passes one copy to either of his two staff, who collects the components from around the building and packages them for delivery, marking off each item on the despatch note. He or she keeps a stock of the courier's *waybills*, which are filled out by hand with the customer's details.

When the waybill has been completed the despatch note and waybill are returned to Dick. Dick checks that all items have been picked and that the customer details on the waybill are correct. He then enters the waybill number into the order on the computer system, and also into a proforma email to be sent to the customer. The customer or Source Computers can use this number to track the progress of the delivery using the courier's website.

They also have fleets of vans to deliver on-line customers' shopping to their homes. However the goods are distributed, it is the responsibility of the distribution function to ensure that the right goods get to the right place at the right time. The distribution function will mainly need to communicate with the production and sales functions.

Key term

Waybill: A multi-part form that is attached to a package for courier delivery. It includes details of who is sending and who is receiving the package and a unique number (often with a barcode) that allows the package to be tracked.

Knowledge check

Who is responsible for distribution in Source Computers UK?

What tasks contribute to the distribution function?

Marketing

The marketing function is often linked with the sales function. It is the responsibility of this function to plan for future sales and to monitor the organisation's relationship with customers and potential customers. One major task for this function will be to advertise the organisation's products or services. This may involve designing advertisements and buying advertising space, designing flyers and arranging for them to be distributed, or arranging for the organisation to have a stand at appropriate trade fairs and ensuring there are people to man it. Increasingly, this task will involve web-based advertising and ensuring that details on the organisation's website are regularly updated. Another task of this function might be to gather customer opinion by arranging for some market research to be carried out. It will be the marketing function that receives and processes the lifestyle questionnaires that we mentioned in the previous unit. In some organisations, this function will be responsible for *direct marketing*, either by themselves or by commissioning a direct marketing agency. As indicated earlier, there will be close links between the marketing and sales functions. The marketing function will also communicate with other functions such as design and production. If the marketing function is going to launch an advertising campaign for a particular product, they need to know that sufficient will be produced to meet the hoped-for additional demand.

Research and development

The research and development function is most likely to exist in organisations that manufacture products but may also exist in some organisations that provide a service. This function carries out research into new techniques, technologies and materials to see if they can be applied to the products or services supplied by the organisation. The development function, as its name suggests, then develops new products or services. This may involve creating a prototype of the new product or service that can be tested to see if there is a market for it. This prototype may never actually be put into production, but aspects of it may be applied to improving the organisation's existing products or designing new ones. For example, car manufacturers often feature concept cars at international motor shows.

These cars feature all the latest developments and are a glimpse into the future. Some features will appear in the car manufacturer's new models, but the concept car in its entirety will never actually be manufactured commercially. The research and development (R and D) function needs to work closely with marketing so that it does not waste time and money on projects that will not match the long-term needs of the organisation's customers. It also needs to communicate with the design and production functions.

Human resources

The human resources (HR) function is responsible for dealing with the organisation's employees. When more staff are needed, the HR function will organise the placing of advertisements and/or notifying the local employment agencies. They will be responsible for sending out application forms and receiving the completed application forms, cvs and application letters. These will be

CASE STUDY 1: FRANCEFILEZ

HR function

The HR function in Francefilez is made up of an HR manager, Nadeem, along with three HR administrators who report to her. This function is responsible for all aspects of the recruitment, training and welfare of staff.

Sales training is one of the major responsibilities of the HR function. They maintain a staff development plan and keep training records for all staff, including sales staff. An independent consultant who has developed a number of courses especially for Francefilez carries out sales training. The HR department uses the staff development plan and training records to identify when a particular sales course is required. They are then responsible for contacting the consultant, scheduling the courses, and ensuring that all appropriate sales staff attend. After the course, it is the HR function's responsibility to update the training records.

Because sales staff are paid on commission, the HR function also has a major responsibility for payroll. When a brochure advertisement has been paid for, the HR function calculates the commission due and adds it to the monthly pay record for the sales assistant concerned. The HR function is responsible for ensuring that all information for the company's monthly payroll, including contributions to the company pension scheme, is kept up to date.

The HR function is also responsible for maintaining the information on the personnel database. They handle requests for staff leave and arrange temporary staff to cover for staff absence or at particularly busy times.

checked and collated by the HR function who will then liaise with senior staff to shortlist the applicants that will be called for interview. This function will organise the interview process and send letters to successful applicants, inviting them for interview. They may also send letters to unsuccessful applicants. A representative of the HR function will be part of the interview panel. When the successful applicant(s) has been selected, this function will produce and send a letter offering the applicant the job. They will also check the applicant's references and prepare and send out a contract.

Other tasks carried out by the HR function will include:

* handling requests for leave

* dealing with disciplinary matters

* arranging cover when staff are on leave or off sick

* keeping record of hours worked and calculating wages due

* organising staff pension contributions

* sending out redundancy notices when staff numbers need to be reduced

* dealing with trade unions and staff organisations

* arranging and keeping records of staff training.

The HR function will need to be in regular contact with all other functions within the organisation as they all include staff who are the responsibility of the HR function. It will also need to communicate with external organisations such as employment agencies and the Inland Revenue.

Knowledge check

Sales staff training is an important responsibility of the HR function at Francefilez. Describe four essential tasks that make up the training aspect of the HR function.

Identify one other important responsibility of the HR function at Francefilez. Describe the tasks involved.

Design

The design function takes over where the research and development function finishes. The design function takes the ideas and prototypes developed by R and D and turns them into designs for the products or services that will actually be supplied to customers. The design function may also design products from scratch, based on perceived customer needs as identified by market research. The design function will need to communicate extensively with R and D, production and marketing.

Production (or service provision)

The production function occurs only in organisations that manufacture products. It is the production function that actually takes the raw materials, parts and facilities and uses them to make the products. In a clothing manufacturing company, the people who perform this function will be cutters who cut the cloth, machinists who sew the garments together and finishers who press the finished garment and ensure it is ready for sale. In many manufacturing organisations there will be a production line where members of the production function each carry out a particular task as the product moves along the line. However, in many industries machines are taking over the tasks, and the responsibility of the production function is more involved with overseeing and maintaining the machines and checking the quality of the products. The production function will need to communicate with all other functions within the organisation.

In service organisations, this function is called service provision. As its name suggests, the responsibility of this function is to provide the service to the customer. The tasks of this function will differ widely depending on the service provided. In an airline, the pilot and flight crew will fly the plane to get passengers to their destination while the cabin crew will look after the passengers by serving them food and drinks and looking after their safety during the flight. In a leisure centre, the receptionist will check members in and hand out towels, instructors will provide classes or individual instruction, and lifeguards will look after the safety of swimmers (see Figure 2.2) and help anyone in difficulty.

There will also be cleaners who keep the facilities clean and maintenance staff who keep the equipment in working order.

ICT services

The ICT services function is responsible for the provision of all computer facilities within the organisation. This will include obtaining, installing and maintaining hardware, managing the local area and possibly wide area network services (LANs and WANs), obtaining, installing and maintaining software and providing hardware and software support to ICT users within the organisation. They will also be

FIGURE 2.2 *Safety of swimmers*

CASE STUDY 1: FRANCEFILEZ

ICT services function

The ICT services function in Francefilez is made up of an ICT manager, Li, and an ICT executive, Mark. Occasionally they contract in extra ICT staff to cover abnormal workloads.

Li and Mark are responsible for maintaining all of the hardware and software of the two local area networks (LANs), one in each of the company's two offices. The network in Head Office is based on PC workstations, with two servers, and the other network is made up of Apple Mac computers. Li and Mark are also responsible for ensuring that WAN communications are maintained between the two sites using a 2GB broadband link.

All of the software used in the two offices is based on standard operating systems and application packages. ICT services are responsible for specifying any changes to these systems that the company may require from time to time.

responsible for internal and external data communications such as maintaining the organisation's intranet and website. Small organisations will probably not have anyone fulfilling an ICT services function but will have a contract with an external ICT services provider to fulfil this role when required. This function too will communicate with all other functions within the organisation, providing they use ICT.

Knowledge check

Describe the tasks carried out by the ICT services function in Francefilez.

Administration

The administration function is usually responsible for the day-to-day running of an

CASE STUDY 1: FRANCEFILEZ

Administration

The main responsibility of the administration function in Francefilez is the processing of customer advertisements after they have been sold. There is an administration manager and three assistants who deal with this.

When a confirmed order for an advertisement is passed by sales to administration the customer's preferred means of communication and method of payment are included. Communications may be by FAX, email and sometimes post; the method of payment is credit card or cheque. The administration assistant uses the preferred communication method to request from the customer the information required to complete the advertisement. This will include a description of the property for rent, sometimes including photographs, availability dates, and prices. The request will include the dates by which this information and payment for the advertisement must be received.

When the advertisement information is received from the customer, an administration assistant checks it for completeness and sends a copy to the design and production department. When payment is received, administration confirms with the design and production department that the advertisement is to be included in the brochure. They also confirm to the HR department that payment has been received so that sales commission can be calculated.

organisation. This may include things like looking after the buildings and facilities, general maintenance and cleaning, fleet management and utilities. However, administration is often used to describe other functions that do not naturally fit into any of the functions we have considered up to this point. Also, in smaller organisations, other functions such as ICT services or HR may form part of the administration function. This function will need to exchange information with all other functions in varying amounts depending on its precise role within the organisation.

Knowledge check

Identify four functions within Francefilez. For each, describe one task carried out that contributes to the function.

Identify two functions within Source Computers UK. For each, describe one task carried out that contributes to the function.

The structure of organisations

As was stated at the beginning of this section, in large organisations the job functions that we have been considering are organised into departments each with a department manager. There may then be higher levels of managers responsible for several departments, and so on.

Such a structure is hierarchical – it is like an upside-down tree (see Figure 2.3). There are many levels of management between the managing director at the top of the structure and the people working in each department at its base, with little direct contact between them. Very hierarchically structured organisations are expensive to run – successive levels of managers will expect to be paid higher salaries than those they manage – and can result in poor worker morale because they are too remote from the decision-making process. There is now a tendency to reduce the management levels resulting in a flatter organisational structure. The extent to which this can be achieved in very large organisations is limited, however, as one person can effectively manage only a finite number of people. Also, in organisations with departments based on job functions, information will need to be passed extensively from one department to another, as we have seen in the previous sections, and no one department manager will have an overview of the task or project. There is, therefore, a need for someone to co-ordinate the work of the various departments involved.

Some organisations arrange their workforce into project teams rather than functional departments. Within the project team will be representatives of the job function required to work on the project. There will, therefore, be less need to pass information to other teams, and the team manager will have an overview of the project.

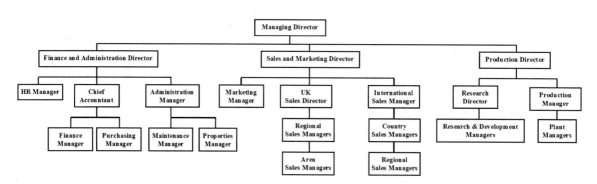

FIGURE 2.3 *Hierarchical organisational structure*

Even in small organisations there will be an organisation structure (see Figure 2.4), although this is likely to be much flatter. The only exceptions to this are the smallest organisations where all the work is carried out by the owner(s) and no staff are employed.

Information and its use

All organisations need information to operate, but some exist solely to gather and disseminate information.

Knowledge check

What term would be used to describe the organisational structure of Source Computers UK?

Who has overall responsibility for the company?

Which staff report directly to this person?

What information do organisations need?

Different organisations need different information, for example:

* a retail shop needs to know about the availability of stock and prices as well as other information

* a manufacturing organisation needs information about the availability and cost of raw materials or parts, the customers for its products and the method of distribution

* a tour operator needs information about the availability and cost of hotel rooms, flights and other transport from its suppliers, and information about booking requirements from its customers.

CASE STUDY 2: SOURCE COMPUTERS UK

Structure

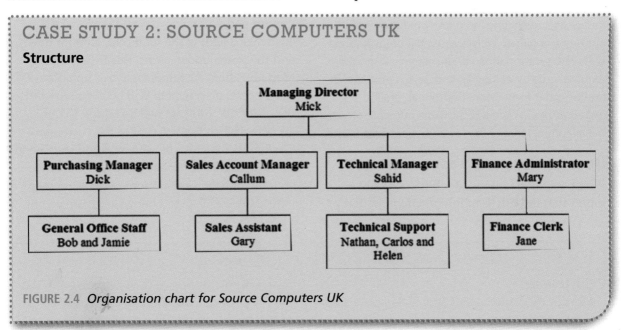

FIGURE 2.4 *Organisation chart for Source Computers UK*

CASE STUDY 2: SOURCE COMPUTERS UK

Information requirements and collection

Source Computers require the following information to complete a customer order:

* customer name and account details
* delivery address or to be collected
* date required
* details and quantities of goods
* method of payment.

This information is usually collected over the telephone, but some orders are collected by email.

Organisations such as news agencies, newspapers and radio and television news channels, along with many others, such as market research and direct marketing agencies, exist only to collect and disseminate information. News organisations, for example, collect the information from many different sources, collate and combine the information to make it more accessible and understandable and then publish the information as text and pictures on paper, as audio reports on radio, as audio and video reports on television or as multimedia information on the WWW.

How is the information collected?

The information needed by organisations will be collected in many different ways depending on the organisation and the information. Market and opinion research agencies will collect information about people's buying habits or preferences by face-to-face and telephone interviews and by sending out questionnaires. Web-based retail organisations will collect information about customers and their requirements by getting customers to complete an on-line order form. More traditional retail organisations will collect the same information over the telephone, face to face or on paper order forms.

How is information communicated?

When we were looking at job functions, we found that the different job functions within an organisation communicate with each other. All organisations will also communicate with people and other organisations externally: customers or clients, suppliers, the Inland Revenue and other official bodies. We will discuss in more detail what information is exchanged between the different job functions within an organisation and with outsiders in the following sections.

Types of information

Customers and clients

Customers and clients will place orders for goods or services. The orders will include details of the goods or services required and customer details to enable delivery and payment (see Figure 2.5).

Some organisations will require customers to make full payment when they place the order, other organisations will require payment of a deposit and will then send an invoice to the customer detailing the total cost, amount due and the terms under which this must be paid. Many business customers may set up accounts. In this case, no payment will be required with the order: the full cost will be added to the account and an invoice sent to the customer. Customers may also be sent monthly statements to show details of purchases, payments made and any outstanding amount owed. Contracts may also be exchanged between organisations

---

CASE STUDY 2: SOURCE COMPUTERS UK

Customers

Most of the customers of Source Computers are locally based computer system builders and small computer retailers. All of these customers have an account with the company, which they can pay by cash or credit card, but more usually by cheque on a *30-day credit* basis.

Account customers generally place orders over the telephone with one of the sales staff. The customer tells the sales staff whether they require the order delivered or whether they will collect it. When an order is confirmed for release an invoice is automatically produced for electronic transmission via email. A printed copy is given to customers who collect their orders but a copy is still automatically sent to the customer by email.

Source Computers also sell to customers who do not have an account with them. These customers can either visit the showroom or place their order by telephone. Non-account customers can pay for the goods by credit card over the telephone or by cash, credit card or cheque in the showroom. However, they will not be able to collect the goods or have them despatched until payment has been cleared.

RKingB **ORDER**

Customer Name and Address	For Office Use
Mr KZ Manlay 33 Woodman Road Gravesend DA11 7QQ	Order No: Date Received:

Telephone	FAX	Email
01474 998647		Kzmanlay@btconnect.com

FIGURE 2.5 *Sample order form*

and their clients. A contract sets out the precise details of the goods or services being supplied and the terms and conditions under which they will be supplied. This will be signed by both a representative of the organisation and the client and will form a *legally binding agreement* between them. Banks and other financial institutions that provide loan services will supply a contract for the provision of the loan. This will set out how much money they will lend, the interest they will charge, repayments the client must make – how much and how often – and what will happen if the client fails to meet the terms and conditions of the agreement. This type of contract also includes items that are required by law, such as a statement explaining that, even if they sign the contract, the client has 14 days to change his or her mind.

Wholesalers and retailers

Wholesalers are intermediary organisations. They buy goods from producers and manufacturers and sell them on to other organisations. They do not usually sell directly to the public. Retailers for the most part buy goods from wholesalers, rather than directly from producers and manufacturers, and sell them to the general public. The types of information that will be exchanged between wholesalers and retailers will be similar to that exchanged between an organisation and its customers. In effect, the retailers are the wholesalers' customers. Retailers will pass orders for the goods that they require to the wholesalers – these are usually called purchase orders to distinguish them from customer orders. The wholesalers will send invoices requesting payment to the retailers, who will then send the required payments.

Knowledge check

Identify four items of information that Source Computers UK needs to collect from its customers.

Identify the two main types of customer of Source Computers UK. Describe the relationship between the company and each type of customer.

What methods of communication are used between Source Computers UK and its customers?

Key terms

Legally binding agreement: an agreement that is recognised under law.
Thirty-day credit: all goods must be paid for within 30 days of the customer receiving them.

Distributors

Distributors are organisations that move goods from place to place. Distributors will need information about what goods are to be transported, where they are coming from and going to, when they must be collected and how quickly they need to reach their destination. The organisation wanting goods distributed will need to know about the cost of the service, how the distributor will ensure that the goods will reach their destination in good condition and on time and what will happen if they do not. This will probably be set out in a contract between the two organisations. Organisations will provide distributors with delivery notes that detail the goods being delivered and the delivery address. Distributors will provide the organisation with delivery confirmations, usually signed by the person receiving the goods, to confirm that they have been delivered as agreed.

Suppliers (of services or goods)

Wholesalers and distributors are two types of supplier. Wholesalers supply goods to retailers; distributors supply transportation services to manufacturers, wholesalers and retailers. There are many other types of suppliers to all different types of organisations. The information exchanged will depend to some extent on the type of organisation and the type of supplier but will often involve purchase orders being sent to the supplier. The supplier will send invoices to the organisation who will then make payment.

Knowledge check

In a previous section of Case Study 2, another supplier was mentioned. Who is this supplier? Who in the company does the supplier deal with, what information do they exchange and in what form?

Manufacturers

Manufacturers are organisations that make products. They will need information about raw materials and parts from their suppliers and will send purchase orders to order what they need. Manufacturers will also receive orders from wholesalers and others wanting their products and will send invoices to request payment. Manufacturers will also need specifications for the products they produce, for new products and for any changes to the specifications. These may be supplied internally from the organisation's own design department or from

Theory into practice

– suppliers

Try to find out about some of the suppliers to your school or college and the information that is exchanged.

CASE STUDY 2: SOURCE COMPUTERS UK

Suppliers

Most of the suppliers to Source Computers are companies who they deal with on a regular basis and with whom they have a credit account. These suppliers are usually the UK offices of computer component manufacturers or bulk importers of components such as RAM and CPUs. When purchasing from importers, Source Computers will usually talk to several before confirming an order, to ensure that they get the best available price, as this is subject to considerable fluctuation. Occasionally, when products are in short supply and their normal suppliers cannot provide what they need, they will order from computer wholesalers to fill the shortfall.

In all cases, when the purchasing manager confirms an order from a supplier, a purchase order is raised by the finance function and sent to that supplier. The supplier will send an invoice when the order is despatched which must be paid within the terms of the credit agreement.

external sources. The information will depend on the product being made but may include precise details about the colour, size, shape and materials to be used. The specifications will also probably include technical drawings.

Managers and employees

All organisations will hold information about their managers and employees. This will include their name, address, education and qualifications, employment history, position, salary, contracted hours, pension rights, etc. The information that is exchanged between managers and employees will differ depending on the organisation and the job function involved. In most cases, however, managers will give instructions to employees about the work they are required to do and employees will report back to managers the outcomes of those tasks.

Briefs

Specifications may be provided in a design brief. A brief is a summary of the specification of a product or service – the term is also used in different contexts by different organisations.

Services

Those looking to buy services will want to know the price and what the service includes for that price. For example, if you are buying an insurance policy, you would want to know exactly what is covered and what is not as well as the cost of the *premium*. If you want to buy airline tickets to Australia, you would want to know the price of each class of ticket, departure and arrival times, where the plane stops en route and for how long, whether you can break your journey there without paying extra and, most importantly, whether there are seats available at a particular price on the flight you want to take.

General information about services will be provided in brochures and on websites. However, clients may need to provide their own information or discuss their precise requirements with the service provider to obtain more specific information.

> ### Key term
>
> *Premium*: the amount of money you pay to an insurance company to provide insurance cover. Premiums are calculated based on the statistical evidence of the likelihood of you making a claim. This is why young people have to pay much higher car insurance premiums than their parents. Statistics show that young people are more likely to be involved in motoring accidents and make insurance claims.

Goods

Customers and clients will need information about the goods that they are hoping to buy. Customers looking to buy goods will want to know the price, availability and the features offered. For example, if you are going to buy a laptop computer, you would want information about its size and weight, screen size, processing power, memory and storage capacity, the software, installed, etc., see Table 2.1. You would also want to know how much each model costs and whether there are any in stock.

This information will be provided in catalogues either on paper, or increasingly on websites. Retailers will also require similar information about goods from wholesalers. However, they may be less interested in the

LAPTOP	CPU	SCREEN	MEMORY	HDD	DIMENSIONS	WEIGHT	SOFTWARE	PRICE
Toshiba	1.6GHz	15" standard	512MB	60GB	365×275×38	3.1kg	XP Home	£1000
Apple	1.5GHz	15" wide	512MB	80GB	348×280×24	2.6kg	MAC OS	£1600
Sony	1.7GHz	17" wide	512MB	80GB	405×280×45	3.9kg	XP Home	£1500
HP	3.4GHz	17" wide	1024MB	100GB	398×288×42	4.2kg	XP Home	£1400

TABLE 2.1 *Information about laptop computers*

INFORMATION	FROM	TO
Orders or purchase orders	Customers and clients	Retailers or service providers
Invoices	Retailers	Wholesalers, distributors and other suppliers
	Wholesalers	Manufacturers, distributors and other suppliers
	Manufacturers and service providers	Distributors and other suppliers
	Retailers or service providers	Customers and clients
	Wholesalers, distributors and other suppliers	Retailers
	Manufacturers, distributors and other suppliers	Wholesalers
	Distributors and other suppliers	Manufacturers and service providers
Delivery notes	Retailers, wholesalers or manufacturers	Distributors
Delivery confirmations	Distributors	Retailers, wholesalers or manufacturers
Product specifications and design briefs	Internal design function or external organisation	Manufacturing function
Work instructions	Managers	Employees
Work reports	Employees	Managers
Goods information (catalogues/websites)	Retailers	Customers
	Wholesalers	Retailers
Service information (brochures/websites)	Service providers	Clients (brochures/websites)

TABLE 2.2 *Senders and receivers of information*

precise specification of the goods and more interested in the quantity available and the likely profit margin.

Key information and supporting ICT systems

There are a number of key information systems that are used by many organisations. Increasingly, organisations will use ICT systems to support these key systems. In this section, we will look at these key information systems and the ICT systems that support them.

Personnel
Personnel systems are maintained by the HR function in an organisation. Information is collected from the employee when he or she first joins the company, usually from the application form. This information will include the employees full name, address, date of birth, gender, marital

status, education and qualifications, employment history, etc. A unique employee number will be allocated. All this information will be stored along with the date the employee joined the organisation, his or her current position, salary grade, contracted hours, holiday entitlement and other job-related information. This information will need to be updated whenever there is a change in employees' details, for example if they move house, marry or get a promotion. It is vital that the information stored is accurate. Inaccurate information may result in an employee being paid the wrong salary or not receiving the number of days' holiday they should. Inaccurate information may even lead to an employee losing his or her job in error. When an organisation needs to shed employees, this is often done on a last in, first out basis – the employees who have joined the organisation most recently are the first ones to be made redundant. If the employee's joining date has been entered incorrectly, he or she may be wrongly issued with a redundancy notice. It is also likely that information about the number of days of sick leave taken will be stored. If an employee applies for a new job or promotion, a reference will be required that will include such details taken from the personnel system. An error may result in the employee not getting the new job or promotion.

This information is also confidential so its security is important. Only the employees themselves and authorised members of the HR department and management should have access to the information held. Personnel records will also be subject to the requirements of the Data Protection Act that you will learn more about later in this unit.

In nearly all organisations, the personnel records will be held in a database on a computer system. The data will be entered from the original application forms and other documents via the keyboard. In small organisations this might be a simple *flat-file database;* in larger organisations the data is likely to be stored in several linked tables, i.e. a relational database (see Figure 2.6). For example, all employees on a certain salary grade are likely to be entitled to the same number of days' leave, contracted hours and overtime rates, etc. Rather than

EMPLOYEES

Employee_No

Surname

Forenames

Date_of_Birth

Gender

Home_Address_1

Home_Address_2

Home_Address_3

PostCode

Home_Telephone

Department

Salary_Grade

Job_Title

Location

Extension

SALARY_GRADE

Grade

Hourly_Rate

Contracted_Hours

Overtime_Rate

Leave_Days

FIGURE 2.6 *Relational database tables*

repeating this information for each employee, if the salary grade is recorded in the employee's record, the other details can be stored in a separate related table with a record for each salary grade.

It is also likely that the personnel database will be linked to the training records and payroll systems that we shall consider shortly.

> **Key term**
>
> *Flat-file database*: a database consisting of a single table of data.

Records can be sorted on different criteria, such as alphabetically by surname, length of service, salary grade or by the number of days' sick leave in the previous year. The records can be searched to find employee records that match a particular criterion, such as those who have been with the organisation for more than ten years. It is also easy to locate an individual employee's record to update it or to use it to produce a reference. Updating is also more straightforward as the old information can simply be replaced with the new.

Training

Ensuring that employees have the skills they need and updating those skills is important to most organisations. This will involve the HR function in organising training for employees and in keeping training records. These will be a natural extension of personnel records. The information stored will include details of courses attended and skill levels reached. Large organisations may also develop training plans for their staff as part of a *staff development plan*. In some industries, there is a requirement for certain staff to update their skills at regular intervals. In these cases, training records are particularly important. Training records may also include details of the particular skills of each employee. This enables the organisation to easily identify employees with the skills needed for a particular project or in an emergency, for example to identify employees with first aid skills, if there is an accident. Depending on the size of the organisation and the extent of the training records, these may simply be additional fields in employee records, or one or more linked tables in a relational personnel database.

Key term

Staff development plan: a document that identifies the existing knowledge and skills of employees and how these can be extended and updated to improve performance. It will allocate resources to ensure that any training provided is relevant to the needs of the organisation and the employees.

Payroll

Payroll systems link the HR function to the accounts or finance function. These systems will have links with the personnel system. Each employee's rate of pay, either salary or hourly rate, and their current *tax code* will be linked to their employee number. All but the smallest organisations will use computerised payroll systems, although some may use an external bureau instead. As payroll calculations are carried out on a weekly, or more usually, a monthly basis, they are often *batch processed*. For hourly paid workers, the hours worked will be entered. This may be done manually or calculated from an electronic clocking-in system that records when each employee starts and finishes work. This too will be linked to the employee number. The calculation carried out will be to multiply the hours worked by the hourly rate. The income tax due will be calculated and deducted from the total, as well as National Insurance and other deductions such as pension contributions. Most systems will then print out a pay advice slip (see Figure 2.7). This will include the employee number, name and address, details of pay and deductions, as well as other information such as National Insurance number, tax code and the payment date. Often, the name and address will be printed in a text box so that the pay advice slip can be put in a window envelope and sent to the employee.

Key terms

Tax code: a code issued by the Inland Revenue and based on each individual's personal circumstances that is used to calculate how much income tax should be deducted from their wages or salary.
Batch processed: processing where all the data is collected or input and then all the records are processed in a single operation. As little or no human intervention is needed, such processing is often carried out overnight when processing power is not required for other operations.

There will be both external and internal links to the payroll system. Externally, there will be links with the Inland Revenue that will require details of wages paid and tax deducted. In most organisations, there will also be links with BACS to pay employees' wages directly into their bank accounts. Internally, accounts managers will need to know the amount paid in wages so that this can be included in the profit and loss statements in the organisation's accounts. Profit and loss statements list all the monies taken in by the organisation (income) and all the monies paid out (expenditure). The expenditure is subtracted from the income to show the profit or loss that the organisation has made.

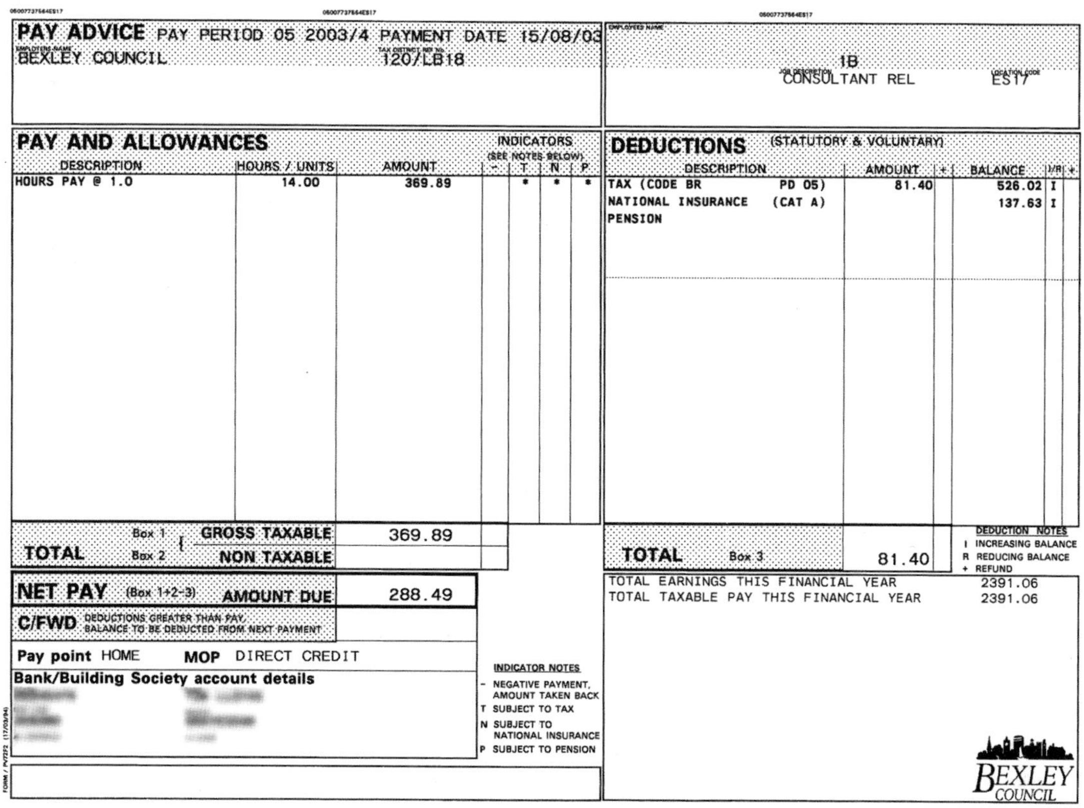

PAY ADVICE PAY PERIOD 05 2003/4 PAYMENT DATE 15/08/03

BEXLEY COUNCIL 120/LB18

1B

CONSULTANT REL EST7

PAY AND ALLOWANCES

DESCRIPTION	HOURS / UNITS	AMOUNT	-	T	N	P
HOURS PAY @ 1.0	14.00	369.89		*	*	*

TOTAL	Box 1 GROSS TAXABLE	369.89
	Box 2 NON TAXABLE	

NET PAY (Box 1+2-3) AMOUNT DUE 288.49

C/FWD DEDUCTIONS GREATER THAN PAY, BALANCE TO BE DEDUCTED FROM NEXT PAYMENT

Pay point HOME MOP DIRECT CREDIT

Bank/Building Society account details

DEDUCTIONS (STATUTORY & VOLUNTARY)

DESCRIPTION	AMOUNT	+	BALANCE	I/R	+
TAX (CODE BR PD 05)	81.40		526.02	I	
NATIONAL INSURANCE (CAT A)			137.63	I	
PENSION					

TOTAL Box 3 81.40

DEDUCTION NOTES
I INCREASING BALANCE
R REDUCING BALANCE
\+ REFUND

TOTAL EARNINGS THIS FINANCIAL YEAR 2391.06
TOTAL TAXABLE PAY THIS FINANCIAL YEAR 2391.06

INDICATOR NOTES
\- NEGATIVE PAYMENT, AMOUNT TAKEN BACK
T SUBJECT TO TAX
N SUBJECT TO NATIONAL INSURANCE
P SUBJECT TO PENSION

BEXLEY COUNCIL

FIGURE 2.7 *Sample pay advice slip*

There are likely to be many changes made to payroll records. These will include staff leaving whose records need to be deleted, new staff being employed so that new records must be added, changes to personal details, changes in pay rates, etc. Like the personnel records, it is vital that payroll records are accurate and up to date. Inaccurate payroll information may result in employees being paid the wrong amount, either too much or too little, or possibly not being paid at all. It is particularly important that tax codes are correct. If the tax code is wrong and too little tax is deducted, the employee is still liable for the unpaid tax. When the error is discovered the employee may have a large bill to pay that he or she cannot afford. Payroll information is also very confidential and must be kept secure, with only authorised members of staff having access to the information.

Design and development

Design and development systems will vary depending on the organisation's specific products or services. In the past, designs would have been drawn on paper by skilled draughtspeople and developed by building and testing physical models. Most organisations designing products now use computer aided design (CAD) systems to design products and 2-D or 3-D modelling tools to test the designs. The CAD systems may even be linked to computer aided manufacturing (CAM) systems to automatically manufacture the product. Records will need to be kept of any new products designed and any changes made to existing products. These records will need to include precise details of sizes, materials, components, etc., so that technical specifications can be produced. Such records may be kept in a database with links to files containing production drawings created using a CAD system.

Purchasing

All organisations need to purchase goods or services. These can be anything from light bulbs to computers, paper clips to conveyor belts, paper to sheet steel, printing Christmas cards to supplying power. The purchasing system will create purchase orders for the goods or services required. One copy of a purchase order will be sent to the supplier and one will be kept by the purchasing function. When the goods or services and the supplier's invoice are received, they can be checked against the purchase order. Purchase orders may be produced on carbonised paper so that the top copy is posted to the supplier and the second copy kept in a file. However, purchase orders may be created and stored on a computer system and sent electronically to the supplier, either by email or by *electronic data interchange (EDI).*

The purchasing system will provide input to the *purchase ledger* in the accounts system. As well as accounts, purchasing will have links with the stock control and manufacturing functions of organisations that supply or make goods. The goods or raw materials purchased will be added to the quantity in stock and the stock control or manufacturing systems will determine when more goods or raw materials need to be purchased as stocks are used up. However, all functions within an organisation will need supplies of one sort or another, so there will be links between the purchasing system and most functions within the organisation. Purchasing will also be responsible for generating contracts for the supply of services.

Key terms

Electronic data interchange (EDI): the exchange of standardised document forms between computer systems for business use. EDI is most often used between different companies and uses certain standards so that the different systems can communicate.

Purchase ledger: the section of the accounts system that keeps records of all the purchases made by the organisation and the money paid out for these purchases. The term 'ledger' is a reference to when accounts used to be kept in large books called ledgers.

Sales ledger: the section of the accounts system that keeps records of the sales made by the organisation and the money paid in for the goods or services sold.

Sales

The sales system is responsible for keeping records of orders and contracts placed by customers. The inputs to the system will be the customer's details and the details of the goods or services required (see Figure 2.8). These details

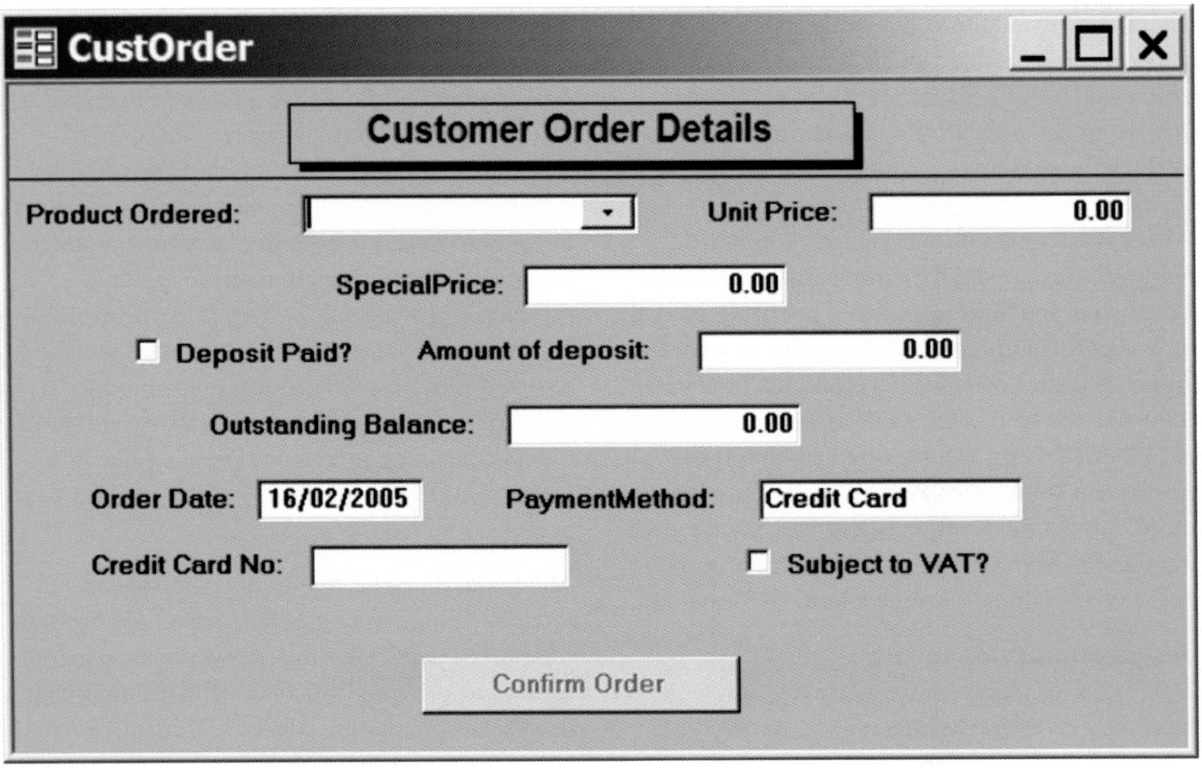

FIGURE 2.8 *Sales order input screen*

will be used to generate internal requests for the supply of the goods or services required. In the case of goods, this may take the form of a picking list, which is sent to the warehouse so that the required items can be picked from the shelves and packed ready for delivery. Delivery notes may also be created and passed to the despatch or delivery department. The sales system will also create an invoice that will be sent to the customer. Most organisations will use ICT for sales order processing. Inputs may be taken from a paper order form and manually entered, they may be entered by a telesales assistant, or by the customer using an on-line order form. The processing carried out to produce the invoice will include looking up the unit price for each item and multiplying it by the number required, adding the totals for all the different items, adding any carriage costs, calculating and subtracting any discounts and calculating and adding VAT. The order processing system will often have direct links with the stock control system so that the items sold can be deducted and sales staff – or the customer in the case of on-line ordering – can have up-to-date information on the availability of goods. The sales system will also provide the input to the sales ledger in the accounts system.

Research

The research function will need to keep detailed records of any new products that are being trialled or investigated. This will include details of the product and of the research being carried out on it. These records will be used to produce reports on the research that will allow directors to make decisions. Analysis of market research findings using spreadsheet models may enable the research function to forecast future trends, such as how long an existing product will remain saleable, or possible new areas that the organisation might venture into.

Accounts and finance

We have already discovered that other systems such as payroll, purchasing and sales will have inputs into the accounts and finance system. The purpose of this system is to keep track of the money paid out by the organisation and the money paid in or owed to it. The sales and

CASE STUDY 2: SOURCE COMPUTERS UK

Finance system

The finance function of Source Computers uses an integrated software package specifically designed for computer companies. Purchase orders are raised automatically by the system on entry of the product details. The system also keeps a record of all purchase orders raised. The system produces daily reports of supplier invoices due for payment and, depending on the supplier, cheques are produced or money is transferred electronically.

Details of all orders are input directly into the sales order processing module. This includes most of the information listed in the 'Information requirements and collection' case study section. However, the only details about goods that need to be entered are the product code and quantity. All other information such as the product description and unit price is stored on the system and retrieved by the product code. Unit price is multiplied by quantity to give a product total. The product totals are added to give a sub-total before the VAT due is calculated and added. All these details are included on an invoice.

When an order is ready for despatch or collection, sales telephone finance to release the order and proceed to issue the invoice. This is done only after the system has checked the customer's account to ensure that payments are up to date. Invoices are printed locally, but the system also automatically sends a copy of the invoice by email to the customer. The invoice total is added to the customer's account.

The finance system automatically calculates and produces the VAT returns for Source Computers. The finance function then raises a cheque to pay the VAT owed. The system also produces information at the end of the company's financial year. This information is sent by the finance function to their accountants who produce the company reports.

purchase ledgers we discussed in previous sections, along with payroll and other financial information, will be used to prepare a general ledger that summarises the organisation's accounts. Most organisations will use ICT systems to keep their accounts. In a small business, this may be a simple spreadsheet or one of the several off-the-shelf accounting packages that are readily available. Large organisations will have *bespoke software* to keep their accounts. The software will be used to prepare a balance sheet and an income statement. A balance sheet is a financial statement that lists the *assets*, debts and owners' investment at a particular date. An income statement lists the money taken in (revenue), the money paid out (expenditure) and the net income (revenue minus expenditure) during a particular period. These financial statements are important to the organisation, as they provide the basis of financial planning so that the organisation remains profitable in the long term. They are also required by the Inland Revenue and by shareholders. To remain profitable in the short term, organisations need to control their cash flow. Cash flow is a measure of the money coming into and going out of the organisation, usually on a monthly basis. The accounts and finance system will keep track of cash receipts and payments so that future cash flow can be forecast (see Figure 2.9).

Stock control or inventory systems

Whilst accounting systems keep track of the money coming into and going out of an organisation, it is the job of the stock control system to similarly keep track of goods by recording the number, cost and place of stocked items. All goods will be identified by a unique serial number. Part of a typical stock record is shown in Table 2.3.

The stock records will need to be updated when goods are sold, by subtracting the number sold. When new stock arrives, the stock records will also need to be updated by adding the number received. As there is a continual need to update the records, most organisations use ICT systems to store them. In small organisations, the updating may still be done manually by typing in the product number to locate the record and then adding or subtracting the quantity.

	A	B	C	D	E	F	G	H	I	J	K	L	M	N
1						Cashflow Forecast 2006								
2														
3		Jan-06	Feb-06	Mar-06	Apr-06	May-06	Jun-06	Jul-06	Aug-06	Sep-06	Oct-06	Nov-06	Dec-06	
4	Income													
5														
6	Product Sales UK	117.20	117.79	121.32	124.96	128.71	132.57	136.55	140.64	144.86	149.21	153.68	158.29	
7	Product Sales Europe	52.30	52.46	52.61	52.77	52.93	53.09	53.25	53.41	53.57	53.73	53.89	54.05	
8	Services UK	9.38	9.42	9.71	10.00	10.30	10.61	10.92	11.25	11.59	11.94	12.29	12.66	
9	Services Europe	4.71	4.72	4.74	4.75	4.76	4.78	4.79	4.81	4.82	4.84	4.85	4.86	
10	Consultancy	24.20	24.32	24.44	24.56	24.69	24.81	24.94	25.06	25.19	25.31	25.44	25.56	
11														
12	Total Income	207.78	208.71	212.82	217.04	221.39	225.85	230.45	235.17	240.03	245.02	250.16	255.44	
13														
14	Expenditure													
15														
16	Product Costs	53.47	53.70	54.81	55.96	57.14	58.35	59.60	60.89	62.21	63.57	64.97	66.41	
17	Services Costs	5.87	5.89	6.01	6.14	6.26	6.39	6.53	6.66	6.81	6.95	7.10	7.25	
18	Salaries	95.20	95.20	95.20	95.20	95.20	99.96	104.96	104.96	104.96	104.96	104.96	104.96	
19	Premises	11.75	11.75	11.75	11.75	11.75	11.75	11.75	11.75	11.75	11.75	11.75	11.75	
20	Other	10.39	10.44	10.64	10.85	11.07	11.29	11.52	11.76	12.00	12.25	12.51	12.77	
21														
22	Total Expenditure	176.68	176.98	178.41	179.90	181.42	187.74	194.36	196.02	197.73	199.48	201.29	203.14	
23														
24	Cashflow													
25														
26	Monthly	31.10	31.73	34.41	37.14	39.97	38.11	36.09	39.15	42.30	45.54	48.87	52.30	
27	Cumulative		62.83	97.24	134.38	174.35	212.46	248.55	287.70	330.00	375.54	424.41	476.71	
28														
29														

FIGURE 2.9 *Spreadsheet cash flow forecast*

PRODUCT NUMBER	DESCRIPTION	COST PRICE (£)	LOCATION	QUANTITY
123456	Parcel tape × 6	0.95	H7	125

TABLE 2.3

Knowledge check

Identify two items of information about products that must be input into the order processing system at Source Computers UK.

What other information must also be input?

From where and how is the information obtained?

Describe the processing and calculations carried out by the system.

State one output from the order processing system and give two ways this is communicated to customers.

In larger organisations, stock control is becoming more and more automated. Product codes are stored in barcodes attached to the item or container (see Figure 2.10). These will be scanned by barcode readers attached to the stock control system when goods are received and sold. This will automatically alter the quantity in stock.

In shops, barcode readers attached to the electronic point of sale (EPOS) terminals are used to scan the barcodes. The product number is then used to find the item description and price for the customer receipt as well as deducting the item from the quantity in stock. Each stock record will include a re-order level. When the quantity in stock falls below this level, a warning can be given so that the item can be re-ordered. Alternatively, this re-ordering process may also be automated. Rather than giving a warning, the system can simply add the item to an order that is automatically sent to the supplier.

We have already suggested that the stock control system may be linked to the sales system. This may be taken one stage further and linked to robotic systems in the warehouse. Each product code is linked to a location within the warehouse. When goods arrive, the product codes are used to identify where each should be stored and the robots are programmed to deliver the goods to the right places. When goods are purchased, rather than providing warehouse staff with picking lists, the product numbers are used to program the robots to select the goods required.

Email

The use of email is becoming more and more widespread as a means of communication within organisations and with outsiders such as customers and suppliers. Internal email obviously requires that the organisation has a computer network, and external email requires connection to the Internet. Where, in the past, managers would have sent memos to staff to inform them of a meeting, for example, they are now much more likely to send emails. There are several advantages to this. The manager can send an email requesting a meeting and asking when staff are available. This needs to be typed in only once, as it can be sent to any number of people simultaneously. Staff can reply with their availability and the meeting details

FIGURE 2.10 *A barcode*

confirmed, all in a relatively short time. Unlike telephone calls, the member of staff does not need to be at his or her desk when the email is sent: it will be stored in the inbox until he or she is able to pick it up. This is particularly useful for international communications when different time zones make scheduling business telephone calls very difficult – 9 am to 5 pm in the UK is 8 pm to 4 am on the east coast of Australia during our winter.

There are, however, disadvantages to using email. One disadvantage is the sheer ease of sending messages. It is not unusual, for example, for someone to send an email to the person sitting at the next desk, rather than just turning round to speak to them. Also, care is needed to ensure information is sent only to the people who need it. Irrelevant information simply adds to the volume of emails people receive. Dealing with this volume of emails can be very time-consuming, reducing the time staff have for their work. The other issue is to ensure that information is not sent to people who should not know it. It is very easy to reply to all the people in a list, rather than just to the person who sent the email. If the email is requesting personal information, for example, your reply might inadvertently provide others with information they should not have access to.

Internet and intranet

Internal networks provide organisations with the possibility of setting up an intranet. An intranet is a network that provides similar services within the organisation to those provided by the Internet outside it, but it is not necessarily connected to the Internet. It allows the distribution of information within the organisation that can be viewed using standard web browser software. The intranet can provide an electronic notice board to keep staff informed but can also provide access to documents, reports and a wide range of other information. Intranets can usually be accessed only by staff within the organisation. However, some organisations give limited access to their intranets to other organisations and the general public. This is known as an extranet.

The Internet provides new opportunities for organisations to communicate externally. Many organisations have a presence on the WWW, in the shape of a website that the general public can visit to find out about the organisation and what it has to offer. An increasing number of organisations have gone beyond this and offer the opportunity for e-commerce. E-commerce is the buying and selling of goods and services on-line. There are some organisations that operate only in this way. A common form of e-commerce is where the organisation sells its goods or services to the general public. The customer selects what he or she wants from an on-line catalogue before proceeding to the checkout page (see Figure 2.11). This shows the items selected, prices, total and any carriage charge. If the customer is happy he or she proceeds to the payment section. This will be held on a secure server and the details entered

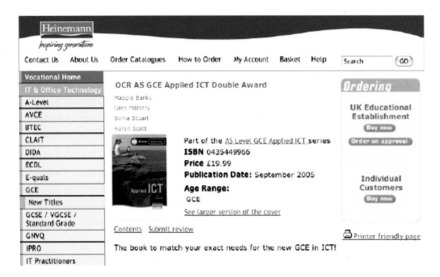

FIGURE 2.11 *On-line shopping site*

CASE STUDY 2: SOURCE COMPUTERS UK

Internet and email

Source Computers currently do not have a website, but one is under development. In fact, their current integrated package is web-based and the website will be integrated into that system. This will allow them to sell their products on-line. A draft of their proposed homepage is shown in Figure 2.12.

As you will have discovered from reading previous sections of this case study, Source Computers make extensive use of email to communicate with customers and between the various functions in the company. They also use Internet banking to pay suppliers and staff.

FIGURE 2.12 *Draft homepage for Source Computers UK's website*

Knowledge check

Discuss the improvements that a website and e-commerce will bring to Source Computers UK's operations and any problems that might arise.

will be *encrypted*. The customer enters his or her address and credit or debit card details to pay for the goods. These details are checked and, if all is well, an order confirmation is shown, which the customer can print out. Often an email is also sent to the customer confirming their order. Goods are then despatched by post or courier.

Another Internet service that is of benefit to organisations is on-line banking. This allows even small organisations to pay suppliers on-line and to move money between accounts.

Key terms

Encrypted: a security method that involves scrambling the information transmitted so that it cannot be read if it is intercepted. An encryption key is needed to unscramble the data so that it is meaningful.

Using diagrams to describe the movement of information

You will need to draw diagrams to describe the movement of information in organisations. A diagram is a helpful tool to make sense of how information moves into and out of an organisation and between individuals or departments within it. This means discovering who needs or uses what information and then showing the links There are many different types of information, most of which we have discussed over the previous pages. These need to be clearly identified in the diagrams, for example:

* customer order
* purchase orders to suppliers
* design and production drawings
* wages and tax-paid details
* records of staff training
* names and addresses of employees
* stock details
* invoices paid
* monthly income

* monthly outgoing

* web publicity pages

* monthly profit or loss.

Your diagrams also need to show the ways that the information is communicated:

* one of the most straightforward ways of communicating information is face to face. This is when the source of the information meets the receiver and either tells or hands the information to the recipient

* information that is on paper can be posted. This can be internal post from one department to another or external post from the organisation to a customer or supplier

* through EDI and e-commerce

* through internal or LAN email or external or Internet email

* the telephone is still a common method of communicating verbal information; this too can be internal or external

* through facsimile (fax)

* some organisations will share information in centralised database systems that different departments can access

* mobile devices, such as mobile phones and two-way radios can also be used to communicate information over long or short distances.

You need to be able to discover which methods are effective and efficient for various organisations, and which methods are particularly effective for various types of information.

It is important that you can interpret a written description of the movement of information during a process, or the movement of information in a process you have observed, and convert this into a diagram. The first step is to identify:

* who sends each type of information

* who receives each type of information

* what is the information

* what communication method is used.

Movement of information

On a blank piece of A4 paper, write the names of the senders and receivers of information in boxes around the page. It is likely that senders will also be receivers of information and that some may send or receive more than one type of information. Each name in its box should appear only once on the page. Next, draw an arrow from the sender to the receiver to represent each type of information. Re-organise the boxes if necessary so that the arrows do not cross. Finally, label each arrow with the type of information and the method used to communicate it. Remember it is only information we are interested in, not goods. The following generic example will help you. The senders and receivers of information are shown in **bold,** the type of information is in *italics* and the communication methods are <u>underlined</u>. The same convention is used in Figure 2.13 to show how they link.

A **customer** <u>posts</u> an *order* to the **sales department**. In the **sales department**, the *order details* are entered into a <u>centralised database</u>, which is accessed by the **warehouse** to make up the order. A *delivery note* is attached to the goods and <u>handed</u> to the **despatch department** for delivery. On delivery, the member of the **despatch department** <u>hands</u> the goods and *delivery note* to the **customer**. The **sales department** creates an *invoice* that is <u>posted</u> to the **customer**. The **accounts department** accesses a *copy of the invoice* from the <u>centralised database</u>. The **customer** <u>posts</u> *payment* to the **accounts department**.

> ## Knowledge check
>
> Draw an information diagram for the process of placing an advertisement in a brochure described in the Francefilez case study.

ICT systems

In the sections on the common key systems found in organisations, we also discussed the ICT systems that are used. Nowadays, it is almost impossible to consider the two in isolation. Even

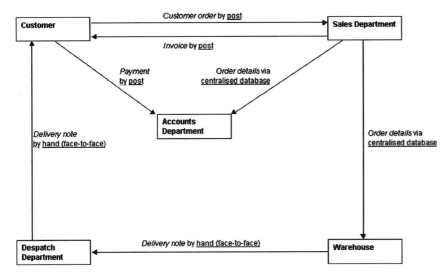

FIGURE 2.13 *Example of a flow diagram*

CASE STUDY 2: SOURCE COMPUTERS UK

Information flow

The information flow when Source Computers order goods from a supplier is relatively simple. The purchasing manager, Dick, telephones a supplier to place an order. He checks that the supplier has sufficient stock and at what price the product is available. He then verbally confirms the order. Dick then emails the finance function with the name of the supplier, and details of the items ordered and an expected despatch date. The finance function sends a confirmation purchase order to the supplier by email. The supplier creates a waybill, which is collected with the goods by the courier. When the courier delivers the goods to Source Computers he or she hands a copy of the waybill to Dick. When the supplier has despatched the goods, an email is sent to finance confirming the date and method of despatch, and attaching a copy of their invoice (see Figure 2.14).

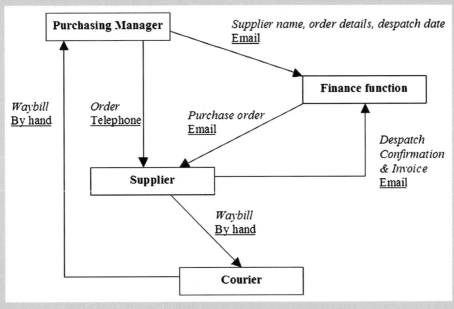

FIGURE 2.14 *The purchasing process in Source Computers UK*

CASE STUDY 1: FRANCEFILEZ

The process of placing an advertisement in a brochure

The sales assistant agrees the details of the advertisement to be placed and the price with the customer by telephone. The customer confirms that they wish to place the advertisement by telephone. The sales assistant then inputs the customer and advertisement details, method of payment and the customer's preferred means of communication into the sales order processing system. As soon as this is completed the order is passed across the network to the administration department for further processing.

Administration requests the information required from the customer to complete the advertisement by FAX, email or post. This will include a description of the property for rent, sometimes including photographs, availability dates, and prices. The request includes the dates by which this information and payment must be received. When the advertisement information is received from the customer by post, FAX or email, administration check it for completeness and send an electronic copy to the design and production department via the broadband link.

The customer sends a cheque by post to the administration department or telephones with credit card details. Administration then emails the design and production department to confirm that the advertisement is to be included in the brochure. Administration also confirms to the HR department by email that payment has been received so that sales commission can be calculated.

---

small organisations rely on ICT for some or all of their key systems and would find it difficult to function efficiently without ICT. When you are considering the ICT systems used by organisations, you will need to identify the hardware and software used, data that is input, processing that takes place and outputs obtained.

You will also need to consider how well the ICT system meets the organisation's needs and suggest possible improvements that could be made. For example, an organisation may use separate and different computer systems in different areas, for example Macintosh computers for design and standard PCs for administration. This may result in duplication of data and the need to manually re-enter data.

Networking these systems would improve the information flow within the organisation. However, the fact that the two systems are different may cause problems and someone will need to manage the network that is created.

Knowledge check

Describe the ICT system used for sales order processing in Source Computers UK. Organise your answer under the headings Hardware, Software, Input data, Outputs, Processes and Personnel involved. (Hint – you will need to refer back to previous sections of this case study.)

CASE STUDY 2: SOURCE COMPUTERS UK

Computer system

All of the staff in Source Computers, except the general office staff, have a PC workstation linked by an intranet to a dedicated server. There are three shared printers in the main office, but both the showroom computer and the purchasing manager's computer have a dedicated printer. All of the computers access the same integrated software package, running on the server, but access to certain functions is limited by passwords. All of the PCs are linked by a broadband router to email and the Internet.

The impact of ICT on working practices

We said at the start of the last section that most organisations now rely on ICT for some or all of their key systems. This increased use of ICT and the technological developments that have taken place have led to changes in the way people work and the types of jobs that are available.

More and more people are able to work from home, more and more people need ICT skills in their work, and new jobs are increasingly available in the ICT field, such as web designers, ICT trainers and ICT support staff.

Location and pattern of work

As was just indicated, more and more people are able to work from home (see Figure 2.15).

This is due to easy access to a high-speed Internet connection and the availability of cheap high-powered computers and peripherals. Anyone who spends most of his or her working day sitting in front of a computer entering or accessing data on a computer network could, in theory, carry out the same

function sitting in their home in front of a computer that is connected to their company's network via the Internet. There are considerable advantages to employers of their employees working at home. Firstly, smaller premises are needed, as there will be fewer staff actually in the office. This has led to a phenomenon known a 'hot desking'. This means that, rather than each member of staff having their own desk and computer, there are a more limited number of desks and computers in the office. Staff who are actually in the office can use any desk and computer that is available. Smaller premises in turn leads to lower lighting and heating bills. This will be balanced to some extent by paying for employees' Internet access, telephone and other expenses.

As well as working from home, people can now work on the move (see Figure 2.16). Laptops enable people to carry their computer with them and work wherever they happen to be. The development of wireless networks has provided wireless Internet access points in motorway service stations, hotels and other

FIGURE 2.15 *Working from home*

FIGURE 2.16 *Working on the move*

locations. These allow people to access the Internet on their laptops while they are away from their home or office. This means they can pick up and send emails and possibly access their company's network while travelling. Mobile telephones allow people to be contacted while they are travelling, both by voice and by text message. WAP-enabled mobile phones also provide email and WWW access.

The ability to work from home or on the move allows individuals greater flexibility in the way they work. There is no longer a need to work from 9 to 5. Work can, for example, be fitted around the family.

Another impact on working practices has come about due to the increased use of robots and automation. This has enabled organisations to operate 24 hours a day. In the past, the cost of employing staff to keep a production line operating round the clock may not have been economically viable. With automation, only a relatively small number of staff are needed to oversee and maintain the systems. Although the initial cost of introducing automation is high, reduced staffing levels and wage bills make 24-hour operation a more viable proposition.

Work skills

ICT has had a huge impact on the work skills needed in the twenty-first century. There are few jobs that do not require the use of ICT in one form or another. In the past, the jobs that required keyboard skills were limited to secretaries, typists, journalists and a few others. Now, a huge range of jobs requires the use of a computer keyboard. If you visit a car dealer's premises, the counter staff in the parts department will use a computer to look up the part required; the mechanics in the workshop will use computers to carry out diagnostic checks on cars they are servicing; the salespeople will use a computer to find out the price and availability of a particular car model, and so on. Where in the past, managers and other senior staff would have dictated letters to a secretary for typing, now they are more likely to send their own emails and type their own letters on a word

processor, only passing them to the secretary to check and put into house style. Apart from using ICT in their teaching, teachers now use computers to create worksheets and other resources and to write reports. All of these people will need keyboard skills.

The increase in the use of ICT has also led to an increase in the need for technical skills. People are needed to build computers and other ICT equipment and to repair them when they go wrong. Going back to the car mechanics mentioned in the previous section, many new cars have computerised engine management systems requiring the mechanics to have greater technical skills than in the past.

Linked with the technical skills required to build ICT systems are the skills of analysis and design. An analyst must be able to study an existing system to identify the inputs, outputs and processing that takes place and whether it can be computerised or upgraded. The analyst must then specify the input, output and processing requirements of the new system or upgrade. The designer then takes over to design the new system or upgrade to meet these requirements. Design skills are needed to design hardware and different types of software, such as applications software, web pages, multimedia applications and games.

Retraining

In the last section we have discussed the effect that ICT has had on the work skills that people need. Some jobs have disappeared or are much reduced due to greater automation and the introduction of robotics, while other jobs requiring these new work skills have opened up. The answer is to retrain the workforce so that they acquire the necessary work skills and can take on the new jobs available to them. For example, some car production workers may be retrained to program and maintain the robots that have taken over their jobs, while others may be retrained to repair and maintain other computer systems. This need for acquiring new skills has resulted in a whole new ICT training industry, which in itself offers new job opportunities for people who have learnt these skills.

Effects on employees and employers

These changes that ICT has made to working practices have negative as well as positive effects on employees and employers.

Social aspects

When people work from home social aspects of their lives are affected. Employees are no longer directly supervised. This means that there is no one on hand to give praise for a job well done, or to push to ensure a job is completed on time. For some, this may result in a lack of motivation and boredom, causing the quality of the employee's work to suffer. Others may be more motivated by 'being their own boss' and not having someone 'looking over their shoulder', causing the quality and quantity of their work to increase. Another possibly negative factor of working at home is the fact that there are no colleagues around to share experiences and discuss ideas. This may result in problems taking longer to solve when employees cannot brainstorm with others, and in employees feeling isolated. On the positive side, working at home gives employees greater opportunities for interaction with their family and neighbours than if they had to travel to work.

Other social aspects of the changed working practices as a result of ICT are the risk of job loss and reduced security of work. We have already discussed the changes in work skills required. This may lead to people losing their jobs if they do not possess the necessary skills. The increased introduction of ICT and automated systems has meant that fewer staff are needed, again resulting in the possibility of job losses. The nature of employment contracts between employers and employees has also changed. Rather than employing staff on *permanent contracts*, many ICT-related organisations employ staff on *short-term fixed contracts*. This allows employers to alter the number of staff as the needs of the organisation change without having to make redundancy payments. However, staff on short-term contracts will lose any sense of security of work, which makes it difficult for them to make long-term plans. Both the threat of job loss and the lack of security caused by short-term contracts are likely to cause stress for the employees

affected. When employers are considering making changes, such as the introduction of automation, they will need to ensure that employees are kept informed and that steps are taken to reduce job losses and provide training opportunities. Failure to handle such issues sensitively is likely to lead to a poor relationship with employees, union involvement and possible industrial action, such as strikes. This may cause stress for the employer as well as the employees.

Key terms

Permanent contracts: employment contracts that have no end date. If the employer wants to reduce the number of staff, employees will have to be made redundant and paid redundancy money.
Short-term fixed contracts: employment contracts that last for a specified time, for example one year.

The balance of responsibilities

Changes in working patterns also change the balance of who is responsible for jobs being done. Employers may suffer stress because they will need to change the way in which staff are supervised and may feel that they have less control over their workforce. Rather than having managers who directly supervise employees, they may have to use tactics such as a performance-related pay scheme or fixed-price contracts to provide financial incentives to ensure employees get the work done. Performance-related pay schemes pay employees for what they actually achieve, while fixed-price contracts provide a pre-agreed payment for completing a job, regardless of how long it takes. Employees have greater responsibility to ensure they carry out the work and meet deadlines without direct supervision and may suffer stress as a result. Linked to this change of responsibility for getting the work done, who takes the blame when things go wrong? If confidential data is lost because computer equipment is stolen from the employee's home, is it the responsibility of the employee for failing to take proper care, or the employer for not ensuring adequate security was put in place? This too may cause the employee to suffer stress.

The amount and timing of leisure time

A largely positive effect of changing working patterns due to ICT is that, in theory, more work can be done in less time so that people have more leisure time. However, the ability for people to access their work at home sometimes means that people actually spend more time working than they might otherwise do. Rather than leave work behind when they leave the office, some people will access their files and continue working when they get home. This is linked to an expectation that employees will be more productive because of ICT, so more is expected of them. Where employees work most of the time at home, the increased flexibility means that they can take their leisure time when it suits them. Some people might stop work mid-afternoon when their children come home from school so that they can spend time with them and then start working again later in the evening when they have gone to bed. Others might take a long break in the morning or the middle of the day, or work through the weekend and take days off during the week so that they can take advantage of cheaper mid-week rates for leisure activities. Even those who actually go to work can often now work flexitime. This means that they have some choice over when they start and finish work each day, providing they work the number of hours they are contracted to over a week or month; and by starting earlier and finishing later some days, they can bank time to take a day, or part of a day off.

The fast-changing pace of ICT developments

We are all aware of the pace at which technology changes in everyday life. Not so long ago, CDs replaced tape and vinyl records as a medium for distributing and listening to music. As the author is writing this, downloading music files over the Internet and listening to them on MP3 players such as the iPod is fast taking over from CDs, and by the time you read this there may well be some new technology for distributing

and listening to music. This same pace of change occurs in the workplace. New versions of operating systems and applications software appear about once a year, each with slightly different user interaction and features which employees must learn how to use. Hardware too is constantly being updated, meaning that technicians and support staff need to learn about the latest components. When we were discussing the changes in work skills, computerised engine management systems in cars were discussed. Every new model of car is likely to have a slightly different and 'improved' system from previous ones, meaning that mechanics have to keep up to date with these developments if they are to service and repair the cars effectively. Wherever ICT is used, systems are likely to be upgraded and changed over time and the more 'leading edge' the systems are, the more frequently these changes will occur. Employees will not only need to learn how to use the systems but will also need to constantly update their skills as the system is updated. It is also then very easy to become de-skilled. If, for whatever reason, an employee does not use a system for a period of time, he or she may forget how to use it and his or her skills may be out of date when they have to use it again. All of these effects of the pace of change of ICT systems may cause stress for employees. The more frequent the changes are, the more stressful it is likely to be for the employees involved.

Theory into practice

– effects of ICT on working lives

In a group, draw up a set of questions to use to interview adults about the effects that ICT has had on their working lives. Use the questions to interview your parents, grandparents and other adults. Share the results of your interviews in your group and discuss the impacts that ICT has had on the working lives of the people you interviewed. Make sure you take notes of your discussions. Individually, use your notes to describe the impact of ICT on working practices in your area.

The impact of ICT on methods of production

In the previous sections on the impact of ICT on working practices, automation and robotics has been mentioned on several occasions. In this section we will consider automation and robotics in a little more detail and discuss the impact of ICT on methods of production. The use of robots and other linked ICT systems has improved production in two main areas: process control and production control.

Production control

Production control involves the systematic planning, co-ordinating and directing of manufacturing activities to ensure that goods are made on time, of adequate quality and at reasonable cost. There are a number of ways that ICT can help in this process. One example of this is just-in-time manufacturing. Using ICT for order processing, stock control and automatic ordering means that raw materials or parts are only delivered exactly when they are needed in the production process. There are advantages to this system. The manufacturing company does not need large amounts of warehouse space to store materials as they can be taken straight from the delivery lorries to the production line. Also, money is not tied up in stock. Raw materials or parts are ordered only when required and they are used immediately to produce the product that is sold, resulting in a minimum delay in regaining the money spent. A disadvantage is the reliance on suppliers and transport systems. If a supplier fails to deliver the parts on time or there are traffic delays, the production process will be delayed until the parts arrive. Just-in-time manufacturing is used extensively in the car industry where the use of robots, rather than people, to carry out many of the processes has meant that the pace of production is more predictable.

Another example of how ICT is used for production control is in the newspaper printing industry (see Figure 2.17). A print management computer controls the whole process. Automated Guided Vehicles (AGVs) are used to transport rolls of newsprint from the lorries that deliver them to long- and short-term storage areas and on to the printing presses. They use sensors to follow a line on the floor according to a program downloaded from the print management computer. The program is downloaded when the AGV is in a docking area where its onboard batteries are also recharged. For safety, the AGVs also have sensors that detect when something or someone is in their way so that they can stop and avoid a collision. As well as controlling the AGVs, the print management computer also controls the production of printing plates, flow of ink to the presses and the cutting, folding and packing of the newspapers. The system even prints and attaches labels for the newsagents who will receive each pack of newspapers. When one press runs out of paper, the process is automatically transferred to another so there is no break in the flow of newspapers coming off the presses. There is some element of process control in the control of ink flow. If you look at a newspaper that is printed in colour, you will see that there are circles of four colours printed somewhere on the page (usually on the fold of a tabloid paper). Sensors check the intensity of these coloured dots and feed the data back to the print management computer so that the flow of each colour of ink can be adjusted if necessary.

Production control techniques have similar advantages to process control. Even if the feedback element of process control is not present, the quality of the final product is still likely to be better than if human workers produced it. This is due to the fact that a robot, once programmed, will carry out a task in exactly the same way every time, resulting in a more consistent output. Human workers, on the other hand, may get tired or distracted and produce output of a more variable quality.

Process control

An example of process control is paper production. In simple terms, paper is made by mixing wood pulp, or shredded recycled paper, with water. The resulting mixture is spread on a mesh so that excess water drains away. In an industrial system, the paper is passed through a series of rollers to remove the remaining water and produce paper of the correct thickness. The introduction of ICT has meant that sensors can be

FIGURE 2.17 *Newspaper printing*

used to test the thickness, water content and strength of the paper produced. The sensors feed back these values to the computer control system where they are compared with stored ideal values. If the two sets of values do not match, the system output automatically adjusts the pulp mixture and/or the rollers to alter the paper quality. Because the computer can monitor and reset each machine hundreds of times each minute, paper quality can be maintained at levels that are very close to the ideal.

Automated systems for process control have a number of advantages. Such processes can produce goods faster than a manual production line and, most importantly, the quality of the final product is higher, as it is being continually monitored and adjusted. This in turn means that there is less waste, reducing the cost of production. Automated production also requires fewer employees, reducing the wage bill, and can continue 24 hours a day without getting tired or needing breaks as human workers would. Processes such as sheet glass or steel production can be very dangerous as they involve handling materials at very high temperatures. The introduction of automated systems means that remaining workers no longer need to handle these dangerous materials, resulting in a safer working environment.

The impact on society

We have discussed the impact of ICT on working practices in some depth in a previous section. As further advances are made in technology, these impacts are likely to become more pronounced. The increased safety of workers due to automated systems was mentioned in the last section. However, the increasing use of ICT brings with it a range of health and safety issues. These include the risk of eye-strain from looking at a computer monitor for long periods of time, backache from poorly designed and adjusted workstations, and repetitive strain injury (RSI) from constantly repeating the same actions. Legislation designed to protect employees from these risks will be discussed in the next section.

Another impact on society of changes in production methods is the level of employment. There was much doom and gloom when automated systems were first introduced, as many expected that far fewer workers would be needed and that there would be high levels of unemployment. Indeed, when automated processes were introduced into the newspaper printing industry, there were large job losses. Now, however, despite more and more use of ICT the unemployment levels are the lowest they have been for many years. Automation may have reduced the number of jobs in some industries, but many new industries have sprung up; for example, people are needed to program and maintain systems. ICT training is another area of growth as is web design, and there are many others. There is, however, a change in the balance of the types of jobs available. It is often the unskilled, manual jobs that have disappeared due to ICT and automation. The new jobs that have replaced them tend to require higher skill levels. People therefore need training in order to take on these new jobs and it is harder for those without training or qualifications to gain employment.

Theory into practice

– automated systems and robotics

Use your school or college library, the Internet and CD-ROMs to find out about other examples of automated systems and robotics being used in process and production control – you may be able to find out at first hand by visiting a local manufacturing company. Select one example of process control and one example of production control and write an essay describing the process and how it has been improved by automation. You should include how ICT has aided the:

* speed of the process
* cost of the process
* safety of the workers involved
* quality of the final product.

Legislation

You will have discovered throughout this unit how ICT is used to store, process and communicate information. This ever-increasing use of ICT has led to the need for new laws. Some of these laws are designed to protect individuals, others to protect organisations and their information. You will need to learn the reasons for the various pieces of legislation, how it affects organisations, and what they must do to act in accordance with it. This legislation needs to be updated to match changes in the use of ICT. The following sections describe the laws as they apply at the time of writing this book. You will need to check whether there have been any updates to these laws by the time you are reading it. If there are, you will need to learn about these updates and take them into account when you are answering questions about legislation in the examination for this unit.

Data Protection Act (1998)

Information has always been kept about individuals by different organisations. In the past, this was kept on paper, in large numbers of filing cabinets, in the premises of the organisation that collected it. To find the record of an individual would involve someone physically searching through the files. It was feasible to search only using the record number or name that had been used to order the records in the filing cabinet. If another organisation wanted the information, if it even knew it existed, the record would have to be copied and sent in the post. If someone wanted to find out or steal personal information, they would need to physically break into the building where it was kept. The use of ICT to store personal information has changed all of this.

Now, huge numbers of records on individuals can be kept on computer. These records can be easily and quickly searched on any criterion, for example to find all the individuals who earn over £50,000. More worryingly for some people, the records can easily be transferred from one organisation to another electronically. Indeed, some organisations exist simply to buy and sell lists of individuals fulfilling certain criteria to marketing organisations. The other cause for concern is the fact that, without good security, personal details on computer systems can be accessed and stolen without the thief having to go anywhere near the place where they are stored.

All of these issues led to the introduction of the Data Protection Act, which was updated in 1998 to cover all personal data, including paper records and not just data stored electronically. Since the introduction of the Freedom of Information Act in January 2005, the Information Commissioner maintains a register of organisations who store and process *personal data*. Organisations that need to store and process personal data must notify the commissioner that they want to be included in the register. The organisation must provide:

* the name and address of the person(s) within the organisation identified as the *data controller*

* a description of the data to be processed

* a description of the purpose of processing the data

* details of anyone that the data may be disclosed to

* details of any countries outside the European Union (EU) that the data may be transferred to

* The organisation must also describe the security measures they will take to protect the data.

Key terms

Personal data: data that relates to a living individual who can be identified from the data on its own or from the data along with other information held.
Data controller: the person(s) who determines how and for what purpose personal data will be used.
Data subjects: the individuals whose information is stored and processed.

The Act contains a number of principles that organisations must follow when storing and processing data and the rights that *data subjects* have. In the Act these are described in detailed legal terms but in essence the eight principles are:

1 data must be collected and processed fairly and lawfully

2 data may be collected and used only for one or more specified and lawful purpose

3 data must be adequate, relevant and not excessive for the purpose

4 data must be accurate and up to date

5 data must not be kept longer than necessary

6 data must be processed in accordance with the rights of the data subjects

7 data must be kept secure against unauthorised or unlawful processing and accidental loss, damage or destruction

8 data must not be transferred to countries outside the EU unless the country provides adequate levels of protection in relation to the processing of personal data.

The rights that individuals have under the Act include:

* the right of access to personal data – the individual must apply to the data controller in writing and will, in most cases, have to pay a fee

* the right to prevent processing that is likely to cause damage or distress

* the right to prevent processing for the purposes of direct marketing – when data is collected by organisations, there is a box to tick either for you to agree that the data can be used for marketing purposes or for you to indicate that it cannot

* the right to have inaccurate data corrected, blocked, erased or destroyed.

Individuals also have rights in relation to decisions that are made automatically; for example, when scores are given for particular criteria and the decision is based on the individual's overall score. If such a decision would significantly affect the individual, for example their work performance or creditworthiness, the individual must be told that the decision was made automatically. The individual can then ask for the decision to be reconsidered.

There are some areas that are exempt from some or all of these principles and rights. This includes areas such as national security, crime and taxation. Some data is termed sensitive personal data in the Act. This is often called confidential information. It includes data about a person's racial or ethnic origin, political opinions, religious beliefs, physical or mental health or any offences the person has committed. There are additional requirements in the Act about processing this type of data.

The Data Protection Act clearly affects all organisations in many ways. All organisations will hold data about their employees; many will hold data about customers or other individuals. The organisation will need to ensure that they register the data with the Data Protection Commissioner and that they take the necessary steps to comply with the requirements of the Act.

Think it over...

In a group, develop a list of all the different organisations that may hold personal data about you and your family. Try to find examples of data collection forms. Look at the 'small print' and discuss how this relates to the Data Protection Act (1998).

Knowledge check

Francefilez collects and processes personal data about the customers who advertise properties for rent. Describe what the company must do to comply with the requirements of the Data Protection Act (1998).

Copyright, Designs and Patents Act (1980)

In the 'Standard ways of working' section of Unit 1, we discussed the need to stop people copying original work and presenting it as their own. At that point, we mentioned the Copyright, Designs and Patents Act (1980). This Act essentially gives the creator of a piece of work ownership of it. For example, the copyright to this unit is owned by the author because it was written by her. If you look in the front of the book you will see the symbol © with the author's name after it. As well as written work like books, the Act applies to many different types of work, including computer programs, drama, music, art, sound recording, films, and radio and television broadcasts. Even the way the pages of this book are arranged and the different font styles are covered by this Act.

The Act makes the copyright owner the only person who can, for example, copy or adapt the work or issue copies to the public. Other people can do these things only with the permission of the copyright owner. For example, where I have used work that other people have created, such as the *Firepower* newsletter in Unit 1, I have had to obtain permission to use it and, in some cases, Heinemann will have had to pay the owner of the copyright to use the work.

There is a widely held assumption that information and, in particular, graphics that are downloaded from the WWW are copyright free. This is not the case – you should assume that anything that has been created has copyright unless there is a specific statement to the contrary. However, the Copyright, Designs and Patents Act (1980) is very complex and does allow some copyrighted material to be used for educational purposes. On this basis, you are unlikely to be breaking the law if you use a downloaded image in one of your assignments.

One type of work that is covered by this Act is a computer program. When you buy a computer program you are simply buying a licence to use it. The person who wrote the program owns the copyright to it (or most probably the company that he or she works for). The licence defines how the program can be used; for example, it will determine whether the program can be used on one computer or on a network and how many people can use it at any one time. A network licence for 30 users will allow the program to be installed on the network server, but only 30 people will be able to use it simultaneously. If you buy a computer program, it is most likely to be licensed for a single user. On this basis, if you make a copy and give it to someone else, you are breaking the law.

The Copyright Designs and Patents Act will affect organisations both as users of copyrighted material and as creators of material for which they own the copyright. The organisation will need to check the copyright status of any existing information they want to use, and apply and possibly pay for permission to use it. On the other hand, they will own the copyright of anything they create and will be able to charge others for using it. The other effect will relate to the use of computer software: the organisation will need to ensure that they purchase the appropriate licences and check that no more than the specified number of people are using it at any one time.

> ### Knowledge check
>
> Describe how the Copyright, Designs and Patents Act (1980) affects Francefilez.

Computer Misuse Act (1990)

The Copyright, Designs and Patents Act is a fairly old Act that has been updated to take into account the changes in technology that have taken place. The Computer Misuse Act (1990), on the other hand, is an Act that has been formulated to overcome problems that have occurred specifically as a result of the increased use of ICT. When we were considering the Data Protection Act, we said that people could access and steal personal information remotely. The same obviously applies to any other data that is stored on computer. The term 'hacking' is used to describe the unauthorised access to computer files, usually for malicious purposes, and the people who do this are known as hackers. Before the Computer Misuse Act became law in 1990, if hackers were caught, it was very difficult for them to be prosecuted under the existing laws.

The other problem that has become prevalent due to the widespread use of ICT is the spread of *computer viruses*. Again, it was difficult to prosecute the people responsible under the existing legislation.

The Computer Misuse Act (1990) makes it illegal to:

* gain unauthorised access to computer material

* gain unauthorised access to computer material with the intent to commit further offences

* carry out unauthorised modification of computer material.

The first two parts of the Act relate to hacking, while the third allows people who initiate viruses to be prosecuted. This part of the Act makes it an offence to intend to modify the content of any computer so that it impairs the operation of the computer, prevents access to programs or data, or impairs the operation of the programs or the reliability of the data – i.e. all the things that viruses can do. Also, the intent does not have to be directed at a specific computer, program or data: again, a feature of viruses. Finally, the hacker or person introducing the virus does not have to be in this country when he or she commits the offence, provided he or she has gained (or attempted to gain) unauthorised access to a computer in this country or the unauthorised modification of computer material took place in this country.

This Act is mainly designed to protect the data and computer systems within organisations, as they are most affected by hacking and viruses, both financially and in terms of the confidence of customers, other organisations and the general public.

Health and Safety at Work Act (1974)

Although the most recent version of the Health and Safety at Work Act became law in 1974, there have since been a number of regulations on health and safety that are also legal requirements. The 1974 Act sets out the duties that employers in organisations have towards their employees and members of the public relating to issues of health and safety, and the duties that employees have to themselves and each other. However, these duties require employers to do what is reasonably practical to ensure the health and safety of their workforce. In other words, the risk needs to be balanced against the time, cost and trouble of taking measures to avoid these risks and whether the measures are technically possible.

The Management of Health and Safety at Work Regulations (1999) made the requirements more explicit. The steps that employers must take include:

* carrying out an assessment of the health and safety risks

* making arrangements to implement any health and safety measures found necessary by the risk assessment

* keeping a record of any significant findings of the risk assessment and the arrangements implemented as a result (if there are 5 or more employees)

* drawing up a health and safety policy and bringing it to the attention of the employees (if there are more than 5)

* appointing competent people to help implement health and safety arrangements

* setting up emergency procedures

* providing clear information and training to employees

* co-operating with other employers who share the same workplace.

Employees also have legal duties. These include:

* taking reasonable care of their own health and safety and that of others

* co-operating with the employer on health and safety

* using work items provided, including personal protective equipment, correctly and in accordance with any training or instructions

* not interfering or misusing anything provided for their health, safety or welfare.

There are also specific health and safety regulations about working with visual display units (VDUs). These are based on and relate very closely to the EU health and safety directives that will be covered in the next section.

EU health and safety directives

In the early 1990s the EU issued a directive relating to the use of VDUs and related computer equipment. This directive gave rise to the Health and Safety (Display Screen Equipment) Regulations (1992). These regulations set out what an employer in an organisation must do to minimise the risk to employees who use computers as a significant part of their normal work. This includes employees who work at home and use a computer for a significant part of their work. This will increasingly become an issue for organisations as more employees work at home, as was suggested in the section on changes in working practices.

There are a number of things that the employer must do to comply with these regulations.

1 Analyse workstations to assess and reduce risk. This includes looking at the equipment, furniture and the working environment, as well as the job being done and any special needs of the individual member of staff.

2 Ensure workstations meet minimum requirements. This includes the provision of adjustable chairs and suitable lighting as well as tilt and swivel monitors, and sufficient workspace. These minimum requirements are detailed in the regulations.

3 Plan the employees' work so that there are breaks and changes in activity. The regulations do not specify how long or how often these should occur but do explain that, for example, short frequent breaks are better than less frequent, longer ones.

4 On request, arrange eye tests and provide spectacles if special ones are needed. Employees covered by the regulations can ask their employer to arrange and pay for an eye test. This can be repeated at regular intervals as recommended by the optician. However, the employer has to pay for spectacles only if special ones are needed.

5 Provide health and safety training and information. Employers must ensure that employees can use their workstation safely, for example by providing training in the best use of the equipment to avoid health problems. They must also give information to employees about health and safety using VDUs, including the steps they have taken to comply with the regulations.

Both the Health and Safety at Work Act and the regulations based on the EU directive clearly have a huge impact on all organisations. Even those with fewer than five employees that are exempt from some of the requirements are affected, as there are still many steps that the organisation must take to comply with the Act and regulations.

Knowledge check

From what you have read in the case study material about Source Computers UK, identify possible health and safety risks to the company's employees and explain what the employers would need to do to comply with the Health and Safety at Work Act (1974) and subsequent regulations.

Sales staff in Francefilez spend much of the day using a computer workstation. Describe how the Health and Safety (Display Screen Equipment) Regulations (1992) will affect the management and sales staff of Francefilez.

Electronic Communications Act (2000)

This Act, as its name suggests, deals with the electronic communication of information. The aim of the Act is to facilitate electronic communication and electronic data storage. One way that it does this is to set up a register of approved providers of encryption services. Encryption services involve the encoding of data so that it is unintelligible except to the people who are supposed to read it and who have the key to decode it. The second way that the Act facilitates electronic communication is by making electronic signatures legally binding.

The Electronic Communications Act (2000) will be of particular benefit to organisations that sell goods or services using e-commerce. It means that the organisation can be confident about the encryption services used to keep customers' personal and financial data secure. It also means that they can obtain electronic signatures from customers on contracts, rather than having to send hard copies of contracts for signature.

Knowledge check

Source Computers UK is planning to use e-commerce to sell computer components. Explain how the Electronic Communications Act (2000) will affect this venture.

UNIT
3

ICT solutions for individuals and society

Introduction

The access to information that has been created by the World Wide Web (WWW) has had a huge effect on society and how individuals live their lives. However, because of the huge volume of information available, finding the information you need is not always straightforward. In this unit you will learn how to search the WWW efficiently to find the information you need. You will also need to find out about the information disseminated by *public service websites*, the increased use of web-based communication by organisations and the effect this may have on people who do not have access to ICT. This unit will help you to find information from databases, use spreadsheets to analyse numerical information and to present the results of investigations and analysis effectively. You will also prepare a report on the sources and methods used to find information.

> ### Key term
>
> *Public service websites*: websites of organisations such as government departments, that provide services to the public.

> ### How you will be assessed

This unit will be assessed on a portfolio of evidence which you will provide. The Assignment Evidence at the end of this unit gives you the ability to develop a portfolio.

By studying this unit you will be able to:

* select *search engines* and use them efficiently to find the information required

* understand the impact of the availability of electronic information on individuals and society

* access information from large websites

* use databases to find required information

* use spreadsheet software to analyse numerical data and present results

* combine different types of data to present the results of an investigation

* evaluate the methods you use to find information and present the results.

> **Key term**
>
> *Search engines*: computer programs that search a database to find the information required, either within a website or on the WWW.

Public-service websites

Public-service organisations, as the name suggests, are organisations that provide services to the general public, most of which have a presence on the WWW. These include:

* government, both local and national

* information services, e.g. libraries, museums, directory enquiries

* emergency services, e.g. RNLI

* the National Health Service

* education

* transport

* broadcasting.

Later we will discuss some of the information available from these large sites. You will need to access and explore the sites yourself to fully

appreciate the information they contain and the facilities they offer. You will also need to download the required information.

Navigating large websites

Many of the public-service websites are very large. Luckily, most provide a range of tools to help visitors find the information they need. It would after all be rather pointless to have a website if people cannot easily find what they are looking for. These tools include navigational bars, textual hotspots, directories and internal search engines.

Navigation bars

A navigation bar usually appears across the top of the web page. It provides links to the main areas of the site and is always visible whichever page you are viewing. For example, the BBC website has a navigation bar that includes tabs for Home, TV, Radio, Talk, Where I Live and A to Z Index. If you want to find out what is on television tonight, for example, a good place to start would be to click on the TV tab to go to the main TV page. Because the navigation bar is always visible, it is always possible to get back to the homepage or any of the other main pages.

Textual hotspots

Textual hotspots are words within a web page that, when clicked on, take you to another part of the site, or even to an external site. As you move the mouse around the web pages, the mouse pointer will change to a hand to indicate a textual hotspot. The text itself will appear underlined as the mouse is hovered over it. The text will indicate what the linked page will contain. For example, clicking on 'find a local school' on the Directgov website will take you to a page that explains how you can go about finding a local school by entering a postcode, with a further textual hotspot linking to the external site that allows you to do this.

Directories

Many large websites provide alphabetical lists of the topics covered by the website. The Directgov website has an A to Z of central government,

FIGURE 3.1 *Navigation bar on the Directgov website*

as well as an A to Z of local councils (see Figures 3.1–3.2).

Rather than having all the entries in one long list, there is a list of letters of the alphabet. By clicking on the first letter of the department you are looking for, you are taken to a page listing just departments starting with that letter. Clicking on E will list Education and Skills and the Environment Agency amongst others. The alphabetical index on the BBC's website lists a mixture of topics and programme titles. Some of the lists for individual letters may still be quite

long and you will need to scroll down to find what you want. On very large websites there may be a second level of index. In this case, if you click on M, say, in the main index, you will be presented with a second list that includes the second letter, i.e. Ma to Mz.

Internal search engines

Most websites of any size will include a search engine that enables you to find what you are looking for. This may be just a simple search, where you type in a keyword and click on the

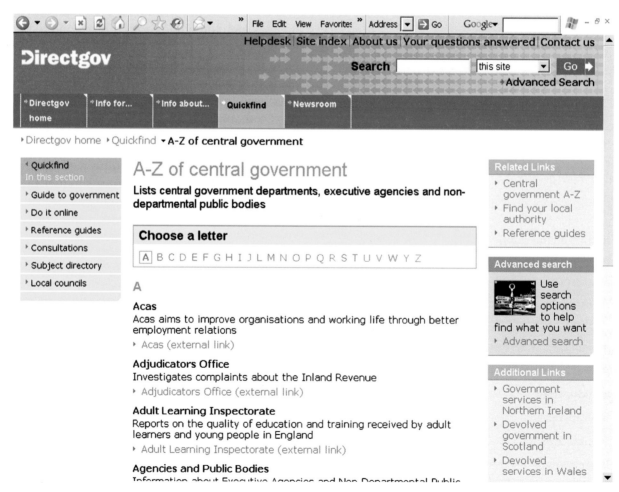

FIGURE 3.2 *A to Z of central government from the Directgov website*

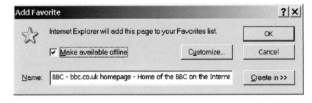

Figure 3.3 showing the advanced search form with the following labels and fields:

What are you searching for?   ▸ Help with word combinations

With at least one of the words [   ]

With the exact phrase [   ]

With all the words [   ]

Without the words [   ]

Or ask a question [   ]

Where to look   ▸ Help with refining results

Search within [this site ▾]

Search in [all text ▾]

From Day [▾] Month [▾] Year [▾]

To Day [▾] Month [▾] Year [▾]

Results order   ▸ Help with display options

Sort by ⦿ Relevance
          ○ Date

[Search ➤] [Clear ➤]

FIGURE 3.3 *Advanced search options on the Directgov website*

search button, or an advanced search facility may be provided. The Directgov site provides such an advanced search facility (see Figure 3.3).

It is possible to search for pages that include at least one word from a list, an exact phrase, all the words in a list or do not include a word. You can also choose where you want to search and to search for pages published between specified dates. Where you want to find specific information, using the search engine will probably be the most efficient method.

Downloading the information you require

When you have found the information you require you need to download it onto your computer so that you can access it without being connected to the Internet. One way to do this is to add the page to your favourites list, and select the option to 'Make available offline' (see Figure 3.4).

Figure 3.4 showing the Add Favorite dialog box:

Add Favorite   ? ✕

☆ Internet Explorer will add this page to your Favorites list.   [OK]

☑ Make available offline   [Customize...]   [Cancel]

Name: [BBC - bbc.co.uk homepage - Home of the BBC on the Interne] [Create in >>]

FIGURE 3.4 *Add to Favourites dialog*

This will allow you to view the whole web page in your web browser as if you were still connected to the Internet. However, you will not be able to move to other pages by clicking on the links. Individual elements of web pages can be saved, copied or printed. Right-clicking on a picture will bring up a list of options that include save as, print and copy. These will allow you to save the picture in your user area, print it out or paste it into a document. If you highlight a section of text and right-click on it, the options will include print and copy, allowing you to print out the text or copy it into a document.

National and local government

A huge range of information is available from government websites. At the time of writing, Direct.gov.uk is a means of accessing any other government website, both national and local (see Figure 3.5). You can find information about local schools, health, employment or motoring; you can search for jobs, find a course or even take a mock theory driving test. A facility offered by the site is to locate and complete government forms on-line. This would allow someone to complete their tax return on-line, for example.

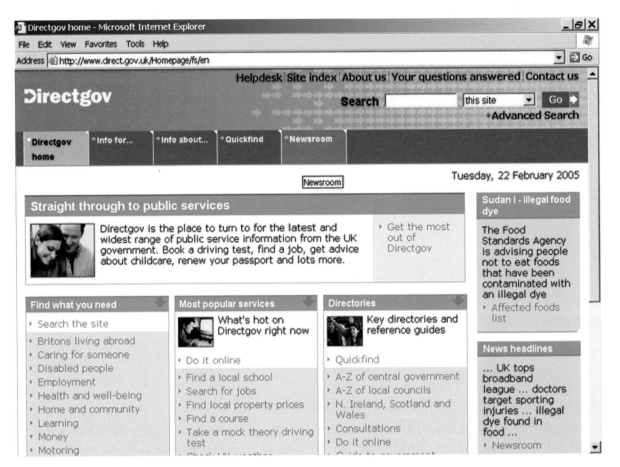

FIGURE 3.5 *The Directgov homepage*

There is an A to Z of central government that provides links to many further sites. Under C you will find a link to the census for 2001 and to that for 1901. Here you can find out about a wide range of population statistics either for the area in which you live, or nationally. The A to Z of local government allows easy access to the website of your local council where you can find out more about the services in your local area.

Information services

Museums' websites will provide information on opening times, current and future exhibitions and any events that they are staging. They will most likely also enable you to view some of their exhibits on-line. In some cases this may take the form of a virtual tour of the museum or video clips.

Library websites will allow visitors to search the library's catalogue to locate books. They may also provide other services such as links to virtual libraries of resources that can be accessed for research or even libraries of electronic images that can be downloaded. The British Library website has a section of virtual books. These are interactive images of some of the many old and precious books that they hold. The software allows you to turn the pages of the book and there is both a text and audio commentary on what you are looking at.

There are many different directory enquiries services available on the WWW. Some of these enable you to find the telephone numbers of individuals or businesses by entering their name and address, or postcode. Others allow you to find contact details of businesses, either by entering the name of the business or by searching for the category of business and the area. Such websites also offer additional services, for example providing maps and directions to show you how to get to the business or even a car park finder so that you know where best to park your car when visiting the business.

Theory into practice

– museums

Access the websites of some museums to find out what services they offer. The British Museum (www.thebritishmuseum.ac.uk), the Natural History Museum (www.nhm.ac.uk) and the Science Museum (www.sciencemuseum.org.uk) are all worth looking at and you will find many more – try typing the word museum into a search engine. Find out the web address of your local library or follow the links to it from your local council's website. What information and facilities does it provide? Finally, visit some directory enquiries websites to see what they have to offer.

Emergency services

The emergency services such as the fire brigade, police and the RNLI (Royal National Lifeboat Institution) provide information to the public about the work that they do and the services they offer. This may include news of recent events or, in the case of the RNLI the ability to see which of their lifeboats has been launched within the last 24 hours. Such sites will also offer information and advice on safety issues, for example how to prevent fires, or the importance of installing a smoke alarm. They will also have a section for those people who want to join the service, explaining what the work involves, what qualities are needed and how to apply.

Theory into practice

– emergency services

Access the RNLI website (www.rnli.org.uk) and a fire service or other emergency service website. Find out the type of information and facilities they provide.

The National Health Service

The National Health Service (NHS) website has a section called NHS Direct. This site offers a wide range of information on medical and health issues. It includes a health encyclopaedia, a self-help guide and a frequently asked questions section. You can also send an enquiry if you cannot find the answer to your problem on the site. The self-help guide takes you through a series of questions about the symptoms you have and will then offer advice about the best way to treat the condition. The encyclopaedia enables you to search for information on different medical conditions alphabetically or by subject, while the frequently asked questions section allows you find the answer to questions on a variety of health-related topics. However, NHS Direct is just part of the wider NHS site which offers information on all aspects of the service. Here you can find details of doctors in your area or which dentists are currently registering NHS patients, for example.

Theory into practice

– the NHS

Investigate the NHS and the NHS Direct websites to find out what information they provide.

Education

There are many organisations that come under the title of education and that provide information on websites. If you look under E on the Directgov website you will find links to many educational organisations such as the Department for Education and Skills (DfES), the Qualifications and Curriculum Authority (QCA) and the Office for Standards in Education (OFSTED). All of these organisations offer information for governors, teachers, parents, students and other people on a whole range of educational issues. The DfES website (see Figure 3.6) has links to a database of the educational establishments in England and Wales that can be searched on a variety of criteria.

As well as these large organisations, other educational organisations also provide information on their websites. These will include awarding bodies, like OCR, who provide details of all the qualifications they offer, local education authorities (LEAs) who provide details of their services, and individual schools and colleges who use a website to advertise their facilities and the courses they offer.

Theory into practice

– education

Access the websites of some educational organisations, including your school's or college's website if they have one. Compare the information each provides and consider the different audiences that the information is aimed at.

Transport

Organisations that provide information on transport include National Rail. The National Rail Enquiries site offers information about the whole rail network in the UK. If you need to make a journey, you can enter where you are travelling to and from, and the date and time you want to

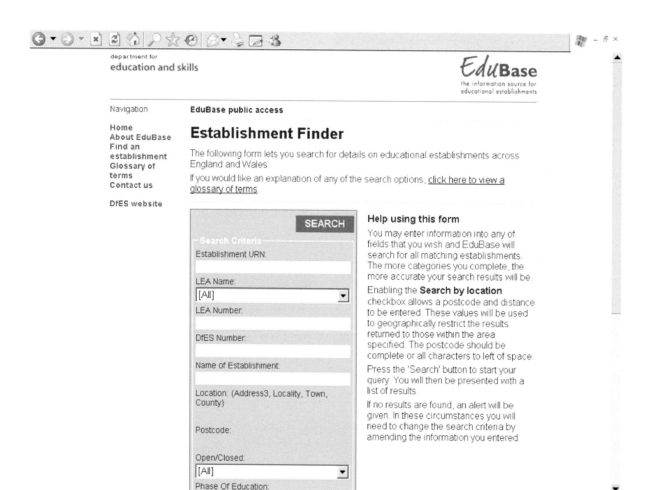

FIGURE 3.6 *Establishment finder on the DfES website*

travel. The site will then provide you with details of the trains that are available and any changes you may need to make. You can also find out if there are any disruptions to train services, such as engineering works, and even access live information about departure times from a particular station that can be updated every two minutes! The individual train operators also operate their own websites. Information about flight arrivals and departures, and airport facilities such as car parking can be found on the British Airport Authority (BAA) website and other airport websites, along with a wide range of other information. Information about bus and coach travel can be found on websites run by coach companies such as National Express Coaches. If you are travelling to London, the Transport for London website (www.tfl.gov.uk) provides a journey planner that includes bus, tube and train information.

For those travelling by car, there are several organisations that provide information on the UK's road network. For example, the Highways Agency site (see Figure 3.7) has an interactive map that shows where there are any problems such as roadworks or accidents on roads in England – there is a similar site for the Welsh Highways Agency.

The motoring organisations such as the AA and the RAC also provide information on road traffic conditions as well as a host of other services such as route planning.

Theory into practice

– transport

Access some websites of transport-related organisations. How would they help if you were planning a journey? Which types of organisation would benefit most from the Highways Agency website? How might organisations use other transport-related websites?

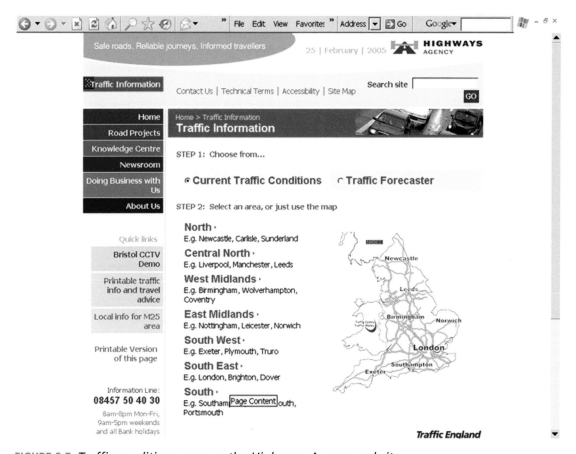

FIGURE 3.7 *Traffic conditions map on the Highways Agency website*

Broadcasting

The BBC, ITV, Channel 4, Sky and many other broadcasting organisations have their own websites. As well as providing information about forthcoming television or radio programmes, most offer a huge amount of information on a wide range of topics. For example, when you were taking your GCSEs you may have used the Bitesize revision guides section of the BBC website to help you. These sites also contain up-to-the-minute news from around the world, the latest weather forecast for your location, the latest sports news and information on a whole range of topics. On the BBC site you can also listen to live radio or to a previous radio programme you missed or want to hear again.

Impact of the availability of information

Anyone who has access to the WWW can access information on almost any topic imaginable; they can also, for example, bank, shop and apply for jobs on-line.

News

In the past, if you wanted to find out about the news, you would read a newspaper, listen to the radio or watch the television news broadcasts. With newspapers, there is an inevitable delay between the story being written and the paper arriving on the counter in the newsagents or through your letterbox. Television and radio news will be up to date but, if you miss something or do not understand, there is no way of going back

to hear or see it again. Also, the finite time available for the broadcast is likely to mean that only the most important news is covered. By accessing news on-line, it is as up to date as broadcast news but without the time restrictions of a programme slot and with the possibility of revisiting the information as many times as necessary. Also, whereas newspapers and broadcast news may concentrate on stories that particularly relate to people in this country or cover them from this country's perspective, on the WWW you can access news from all over the world and from other people's perspectives. This gives individuals the opportunity to gain a more balanced view of what is happening in the world than they would have otherwise. This may eventually lead to a more tolerant society, but this seems a long way off.

National and local government websites

Access to national and local government websites makes it easier for people to find out about issues that affect their daily lives. As this is being written, there is a problem regarding a banned additive that has found its way into a wide range of prepared foods. A visit to the Food Standards Agency website has quickly provided a list of all the foods that have been affected and which should not be eaten. Parents choosing which primary or secondary school their child will attend can access information on performance tables, read OfSTED reports and find the contact details of schools in their area. This increased availability of information can lead to some schools becoming over-subscribed, while others suffer from falling pupil numbers.

It can also lead to increased pressure on schools and teachers to improve performance. In some areas, parents have been known to move house, with an associated increase in house prices, so that their children can go to a popular high-performing school.

Banking

Banking is another area that has been hugely affected by the WWW. Where in the past you would know the state of your account only when you received your monthly statement or if you went into your branch to ask, now you can gain access to your bank statement on-line at any time and from anywhere. You can also transfer money between your own accounts, transfer money to other people's accounts and pay bills. These are all tasks that in the past could be done only by going into the bank branch or writing and posting a cheque. Internet banking means that individuals are much better informed about their financial position and can manage their money much more easily.

Travel

Travel too has been affected by the availability of information on-line. In the past, information on train times, for example, was available only from often complex printed train timetables or by telephoning the rail enquiries service. Similarly, information on any disruption to services could be obtained only from notices in affected stations or from the rail enquiries telephone line, which was often busy. The National Rail Enquiries website and those of the individual train operators can provide all this information in an easy-to-access way. Instead of having to locate information in complex timetables and having to work out any connections yourself, you can simply enter the start and end points of the journey and the date and time you want to travel. The website will then provide details of suitable trains, how long it will take and where you need to change trains. Some sites then allow you to book tickets on-line, often at reduced prices. When travelling by car, websites allow you to plan your route to avoid roadworks and you can check before leaving whether there are any accidents or traffic congestion that will affect your journey.

On-line shopping

As well as train tickets, you can buy almost anything on-line. Groceries, clothes, furniture, toys, films and much more can be bought from websites offering e-commerce. As well as this, auction sites allow individuals to sell items on the WWW. On-line shopping offers many benefits to consumers. You can shop around for the best price without wasting shoe leather or petrol visiting different stores. People who are housebound or have difficulty getting to shops can buy on-line and have their purchases delivered to their door. Companies often offer extra discount to on-line shoppers, saving them more money. Also, you are not limited to the shops available in your local area; you can buy goods from companies located anywhere in the country or even overseas.

There are, however, some limitations to shopping on-line. You will almost always have to supply a credit or debit card number to pay for your purchases, making the experience of shopping on-line out of reach to people who do not have one. Some people are also concerned about the security of their personal and credit card details being transmitted. Particularly with auction sites, you may not be sure whether what you have bought will arrive or not, or whether it will be what you expected – although most auction sites have safeguards against this. You can see only the pictures of the goods on-screen, you cannot handle them or, in the case of clothes, try them on. However, most websites will allow you to return the goods if they do not meet your requirements, often without charge. The increase in on-line shopping also affects society. The more people shop on-line, the less they visit high street shops. This may result in the closure of some high street outlets, resulting in less choice for those who do not have access to on-line shopping. This may also result in a reduction in the number of retail jobs, but the number of jobs in other areas, such as courier services will increase.

Impact on methods of communication

Increased access to the WWW has led to changes in the way that organisations communicate with their clients or customers and with society in general. The prime minister has said that all priority public services, both national and local, should be available on-line by the end of 2005. There is currently an e-government unit that is responsible for ensuring that this target is met. One of their initiatives was the Directgov website that we discussed earlier in this unit. Already it is possible to carry out a range of communications with central and local government departments on-line. Until this year (2004/5), voter registration forms had to be completed by hand and posted back to the local council. This year the process could be completed on-line by visiting the local council's website. It is also possible to apply for a passport, book a driving test, complete your tax return and pay for a TV licence on-line. You can even report a minor crime on-line. In the local elections of 2002, some councils piloted e-voting, allowing people to cast their vote on a secure website. Such pilots are likely to become more widespread in future, partly as it is felt this will encourage more younger people to cast their vote.

> ### Key term
>
> *Utility companies*: companies that provide utilities such as water, electricity, gas and telephone services.

It is not just government that is increasingly using web-based communication. Utility companies too are encouraging customers to communicate with them on-line. Gas and electricity companies offer self-read schemes, where customers take their own meter reading and send it in. Often, extra discounts are offered if the reading is input on the company's website. Such companies are also offering customers on-line billing. This means that, rather than receiving a paper bill, when the bill is due the customer is sent an email so that they can visit the company's website and view and pay their bill on-line. All of these communications initiatives save the companies money. If readings are submitted on-line, the companies do not have to pay someone to enter them, while electronic bills reduce the cost of paper to print them and postage to send them. Banks too are offering the option of not sending paper statements through the post to those who bank on-line.

Effects on people who do not have access to ICT

Figures from the Office of National Statistics show that, by the end of 2003, 49 per cent of households in the UK had home access to the Internet. However, when this is broken down by income,

only 12 per cent of those in the lowest income band have home access, while the figure is 85 per cent for the highest income band. Age too is a factor when it comes to Internet access. Although by July 2004, 60 per cent of adults said that they had used the Internet, for 16- to 24-year-olds this figure is 91 per cent, falling to 50 per cent for 55- to 64-year-olds, and below 20 per cent for those who are 65 or older. Whilst these figures have increased rapidly since 1998 (only 9 per cent of households had home Internet access at that time), the increase has been slowest for the lowest income households and the oldest individuals.

If national and local government are increasingly offering on-line services, it is the people who are most likely to need those services who do not have access to ICT and the Internet. Earlier in this section, we mentioned a problem with an illegal additive getting into a wide range of prepared foods. Although this was widely reported in the press and on television, most of these reports referred people to the Food Agency's website to find out exactly which products were affected. This clearly has implications for those people who do not have Internet access. Current affairs programmes on the television, when discussing issues that are important to the less advantaged members of society then refer viewers to a website for further information. Again, it is the people who would benefit most from this information who are least likely to have access to it.

Alongside the push to get public services on-line, there are initiatives to provide Internet access to those who do not have it at home. An initiative in England and Wales called 'The People's Network' aims to make sure that every public library in England and Wales is linked to the Internet and has enough funding for computers so that people can access the Internet in their local library. Another initiative called 'everybodyonline' aims to increase access to ICT and the Internet in disadvantaged communities across the country. However, such initiatives also need to overcome people's resistance to using the Internet. The latest available figures from the Office of National Statistics (July 2004) show that 48 per cent of people who have never used the

Internet do not want to, need to or have an interest in doing so, while a further 14 per cent felt it offered no benefits to them. Only 37 per cent cited not having an Internet connection as the reason for not using it. All of the figures quoted here are the latest available at the time of writing. By the time you read this, the situation may have changed. You can check this out for yourself by going to the Office of National Statistics' website. There is a link under S on the Directgov website.

Think it over...

When you have spent some time investigating public-service websites, discuss in a group the types of information available and how access to this information might affect individuals and society. Carry out your own survey to find out who uses/has access to the Internet and who does not. Compare your findings to the figures nationally. Discuss in your group the impact on people who do not have access to ICT of the increased use of the Internet by organisations to communicate information.

Search engines

The WWW can be a powerful tool when used for searching for information, especially when search engines are utilised correctly.

What is a search engine?

A search engine is a computer program that searches a very large database to locate the information required. We have already said that large websites, such as the Directgov website, have search engines that allow you to search the site for the information you need. There are similar search engines that allow you to search the WWW to find specific information. The databases for these search engines contain extracts from millions of web pages, along with associated keywords and the location of each page. In most cases, the data on the different web pages is collected automatically using programs that search the WWW for new sites and add them to the database. The BBC website, as well as providing a search engine to search within the site, also allows searches to be made of the WWW. In this case, there is some human intervention in determining the content of the database, both in checking that inappropriate sites are not included and in providing a list of recommended sites.

Search engines allow you to find web pages via their content. When you type what you want to find into the search engine, the database is searched to find all the pages containing the word(s) you have entered. The search engine will then display extracts from the pages found that contain these word(s), and hyperlinks to take you to the page. The pages will be listed by the number of 'hits' they have received, with the most popular first. If you enter two or more words, the search engine may return pages that contain the words separately, rather than as you typed them, pages with the words in a different order, or pages that contain only some of the words. For example, a search for plant house returned pages about houseplants, several references to House of Commons/Lords proceedings that mentioned plant, and even a page on the history of astrology where the author's surname was Plant and the text included the word house. One way to overcome this is to put speech marks round the phrase that you want to find. Searching for 'plant house' reduced the number of hits from over a million to just under 2000, all of which included the exact phrase plant house. We will consider other ways of adding precision to searches later in this section.

The range of search engines

There are a number of different web search engines, for example Google, Yahoo, Alta Vista, Ask Jeeves, to name but a few. These are all general search engines that can be used to search for any topic. Ask Jeeves is a little different from the other three, as it allows you to actually type a question such as 'how do you create a website'. This will return a list of references related to building a website. If you enter a question that asks 'what is...' a definition may also be provided, while questions that ask 'who was/is...' may provide a picture and some biographical details about the person. As well as these general search engines, there are specialist search engines, for example for scientific material, fine arts, music downloads, shopping, and many other areas. Some search engines are designed specifically for children, while others combine results from a number of different search engines. There are also search engines that relate to specific countries. Most websites return the results in a similar way, but there is at least one search engine that displays the results as a sort of mind map that allows you to narrow down the search by selecting topics.

Results from different search engines

The results you get from different search engines will depend on the database used. Some search engines, known as meta-search engines, do not have their own database of web pages. Instead, they transmit your search to several individual

search engines and their databases. You then get back results from all the search engine databases queried. This should, in theory, give better results than searches using an individual search engine. However, meta-search engines do not always have access to the largest and most useful search engine databases, relying instead on small free search engines and directories which give fewer results. Table 3.1 shows the results obtained from different search engines when the same search was carried out. In all cases, the text entered was Pentium 4 system.

SEARCH ENGINE	NUMBER OF HITS
Google	9,180,000
Yahoo	11,700,000
MSN	2,351,796
Ask Jeeves	1,978,000
WebCrawler	76
Dogpile	84

TABLE 3.1 *Search engine results*

The most striking difference is that the first four of these have hit rates measured in millions, while the last two returned less than 100 hits each. The first four are all individual search engines with their own databases; the last two are both meta-search engines.

Which search engine is best?

Which search engine you use for which purpose is, to some extent, a matter of personal preference. However, as we have just discovered, the results from different search engines are not all the same. Some things to consider when choosing which search engine to use include the subject area you are searching for, what type of media you are searching for and where you are located in the world or which part of the world you want to find out about. If you want to find out about anything that is UK-based, you need to make sure that you use a UK-based search engine, or the UK version of an international one. If you choose google.co.uk rather than google.com, ask.co.uk rather than ask.com or uk.yahoo.com rather than just yahoo.com, you will access the UK version of each search engine and will be given the option to just search UK pages. This means, for example, that if you search for 'football' you will get results relating only to soccer, rather than to American football. The best way to find out which search engine to use is to try the same search in different search engines to find which gives the most useful results.

– different search engines

Enter the same search in a number of different search engines and compare the results you obtain. Compare searches of UK sites and the web from UK-based search engines with the same searches carried out in US-based search engines or those based in other countries.

To add precision to a search you will need to use facilities such as logical operators and advanced search options.

Logical operators (AND, OR, NOT)

Logical operators are AND, OR and NOT. These can be used to add precision to the searches you make using search engines. The way that they work can best be described using an example. This is shown in Table 3.2. All searches were carried out using google.co.uk, searching UK-based sites only.

Using the AND operator narrows down the search. The more words you include, the narrower the search becomes. The OR operator, on the other hand, widens the search. In some search engines, such as Google, it is not necessary to actually enter the word AND between search words, as the search engine includes all the search terms entered by default. In other words, it assumes that you want all the words you type

SEARCH CRITERION	WHAT IT LOOKS FOR	NUMBER OF HITS
Museum	Any pages that contain the word museum	7,540,000
Museum AND science	Pages that contain both the words museum AND science	3,410,000
Museum AND science AND technology	Pages that contain all three search words	1,120,000
Museum AND science AND technology AND London	Pages that contain all four search words	479,000
Museum AND science AND technology AND London AND industry	Pages that contain all five search words	267,000
Museum AND science AND technology AND London AND industry AND medicine	Pages that contain all six search words	158,000
Museum AND science NOT technology	Pages that contain the words museum AND science but NOT the word technology	1,980,000
Museum OR technology	Pages that contain either the word museum OR the word technology	18,900,000

TABLE 3.2 *The effect of using logical operators*

in to appear on all the hits. In other search engines you may need to use the operator if you want only pages containing all the words you enter. The other point to note from the table is that Google uses a minus sign to represent the NOT operator. This is also the case with some other search engines.

Advanced search options

Another way of adding precision to searches is to use the advanced search options offered by the search engine. You have already seen an example of an advanced search option within the Directgov website. Web search engines offer similar advanced options.

Some of the options offered in the advanced search on google.co.uk (see Figure 3.8) are the same as using the logical operators we have just been looking at. The option 'with all the words' is the same as the AND operator. Earlier we mentioned putting speech marks around two or more words to ensure that results contained only

the exact phrase. The option 'with the exact phrase' has the same effect. The option 'with at least one of the words' is the same as using the OR operator, while 'without the words' is the same as using the NOT operator.

As well as these logical options, search engines offer further advanced options to help you make your search more precise. For example, you can request that **only** pages written in a particular language are returned, for example only those written in English. You can request that the search engine returns only results that have a particular file format, for example only those in Rich Text Format (.rtf) or Adobe Acrobat format (.pdf), or you can request that results **do not** have a particular file format. As it is very easy to find information that is out of date on the WWW, a useful option is to request that the search engine returns only results that have been updated in a specified period, for example in the past three months, six months or year. You can choose where on the web pages your search term must appear,

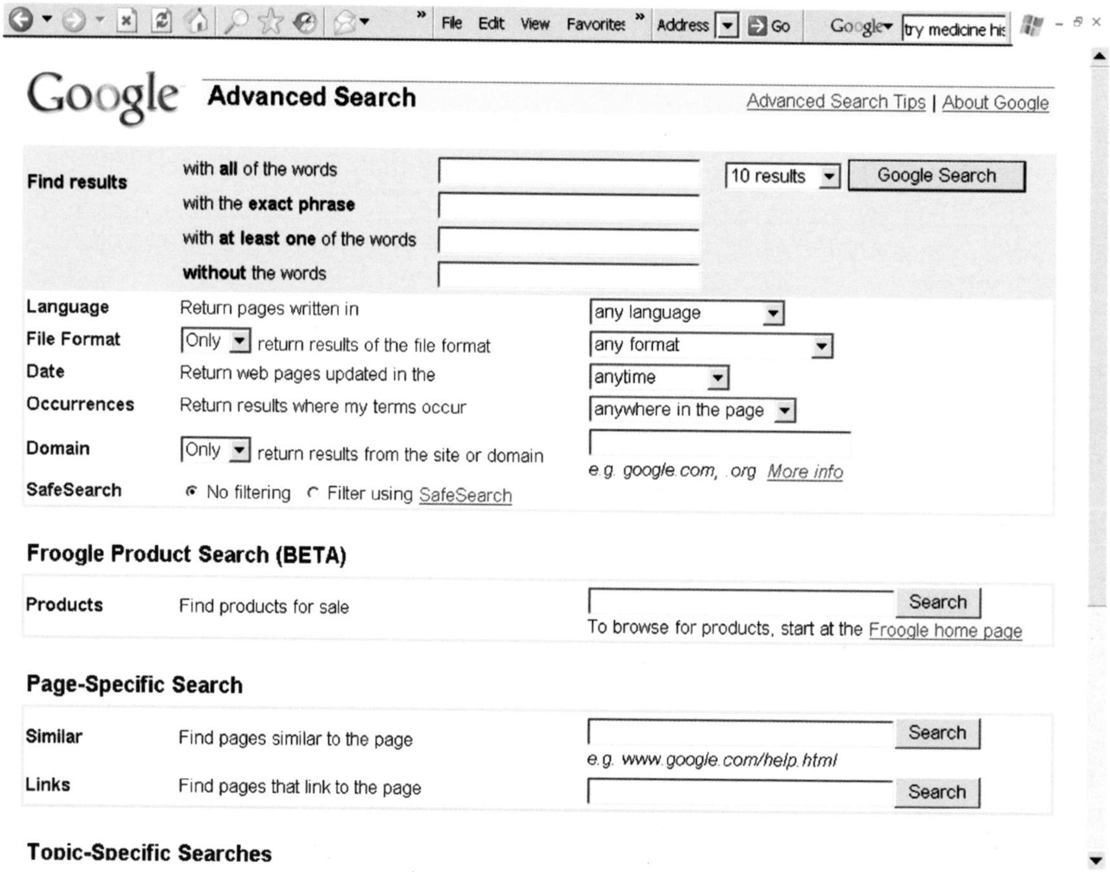

FIGURE 3.8 *Advanced search option in google.co.uk*

for example in the title, in the text or in the *URL*. You can request that only a particular site or a particular domain is searched, for example search only direct.gov.uk, or only sites that have the domain .ac.uk. You can also exclude particular sites or domains from your search. Although the advanced options described are those offered by google.co.uk, most other search engines will offer similar options, although these may appear in a different way. Advanced search options may also offer the facility to filter the search results so that inappropriate websites are not included.

Theory into practice

– logical operators

Use logical operators to carry out searches for information on the WWW. Compare the advanced search options offered by different search engines. Use the advanced search options in different search engines to search for information. Compare the results obtained using similar options in different search engines to carry out the same search.

✳ REMEMBER!

✳ Search engines are computer programs that allow large databases to be searched to find the information required.

✳ Web search engines use databases that include extracts from millions of web pages.

✳ There are many different search engines available, which may generate different results from the same search.

✳ When choosing a search engine, you should consider subject area, media and location.

✳ Facilities exist to add precision to searches, including logical operators (AND, OR, NOT) and advanced search options.

Databases

A database is simply a collection of data stored on a computer system in some organised way so that it is easy to retrieve information based on particular search criteria. We have already discovered that search engines use databases to locate information and that some websites include databases that can be searched, for example the educational establishment database on the DfES website. These are large on-line databases. Organisations use databases to store personnel records (see Figure 3.9), customer records, stock records, etc. The size of these databases will depend on the size of the organisation. They will most probably be stored on the server of the organisation's network. Although you do not have to know how to create a database for this unit, you may have created your own databases in the past, or your teacher may provide databases that are stored locally for you to search. These are likely to be relatively small databases. You may also find databases stored on CD-ROM.

In order to search databases effectively, you need to know something about how databases are structured. A database consists of one or

Field Name	Data Type
EmployeeID	AutoNumber
Surname	Text
First Name	Text
Addr1	Text
Addr2	Text
Addr3	Text
Post-code	Text
Tel No	Text
Position	Text
Contract	Text
Plumber/ Carpenter/ Electrician	Text
Annual Salary	Currency
Normal hours	Number
Hourly rate	Currency
Overtime rate	Currency
Commission Rate	Text
Date of Birth	Date/Time
N I Number	Text
Tax Code	Text
Holiday Entitlement	Number
Pension Scheme	Yes/No

FIGURE 3.9 *Fields in a personnel database*

more tables of data. All the data in a table will be about one subject, for example employees, customers or products. Each row in the table, which is known as a record, will contain all the data about one person or object, for example one employee, customer or product. Each record contains a number of fields, each of which contains an individual item of data. These are the column headings in the table. All records contain the same fields. Fields in a database of customers could include: surname, title, initial, address (usually broken down into several fields) telephone number, etc.

Searching a database involves looking for particular values in one or more fields. The result will include all the records that match the search criterion. Large on-line databases are likely to have a built-in search engine to help you find the information you are looking for. The educational establishment database on the DfES website allows you to enter what you know about the school or college you are searching for. The more you can enter, the more accurate your search is likely to be. You can also restrict the search to establishments within a certain distance of the postcode you enter. As such databases are designed to be used by the general public, there will often be easy to follow instructions on how to carry out a search. Databases used in organisations will usually have been set up so that the database's structure is hidden from the people using it. There are likely to be ready set-up queries and reports that allow the users to extract the information they need. However, if you are searching a local database you will need to know how to set up

your own search criteria and output the results in a report format.

Searches using a single criterion

The simplest way to search a database is to look for one particular item of data within one field. An example would be to find all the employees with a particular tax code in the personnel database shown in Figure 3.10. One way to do this is to select one instance of the value you require and use the filter by selection button. This will leave just records with that particular tax code. However, this is a rather inflexible way to search, as it does not allow you to select which fields within the records you want to display or to display the results in a report. A better way to search the database is to set up a query.

Only the fields employee, ID, surname, first name, position, NI number and tax code will be displayed in the results as demonstrated in Figure 3.11.

Searches using relational operators

Relational operators include equal to (=), greater than (>), less than (<), not equal to (<>), is the same as, comes before and comes after. The last three are usually used to search fields containing textual data, while the others are usually used to search fields containing numerical data, although the first three and the last three are essentially the same. The search for a tax code uses the = or 'is the same as' operator. To find all employees who earn more than £15,000 per year requires the Annual Salary field to be added to the query with the criterion >15000. The results are shown in Figure 3.12.

Field:	EmployeeID	Surname	First Name	Position	NI Number	Tax Code	
Table:	Personnel	Personnel	Personnel	Personnel	Personnel	Personnel	
Sort:							
Show:	☑	☑	☑	☑	☑	☑	
Criteria:						"L372"	
or:							

FIGURE 3.10 *A query to find employees with the tax code L372*

EmployeeID	Surname	First Name	Position	N I Number	Tax Code
3	Hill	Phyllis	Sales Grade B	IJ289001H	L372
8	Ricketts	Diane	Sales Grade A	GW121905M	L372
9	Croker	Susan	Cashier	LD864120V	L372
11	Findlater	Martin	Contractor	RA890466D	L372
17	Nicholls	Amanda	Contractor	SC567420A	L372
19	Pyrda	Nana	Sales Grade C	BA560963D	L372
21	Han	Yueng	Sales Grade B	HA445890D	L372
*	(AutoNumber)				

FIGURE 3.11 *Results of tax code query*

EmployeeID	Surname	First Name	Position	Annual Salary
1	McNamara	Patrick	Sales Grade A	£18,200.00
3	Hill	Phyllis	Sales Grade B	£20,000.00
6	Dudley	Nigel	Sales Manager	£28,750.00
8	Ricketts	Diane	Sales Grade A	£17,900.00
12	Lodge	John	Sales Grade C	£21,200.00
14	Smith	Anita	Sales Grade A	£17,900.00
18	Abdullah	Mohammed	Sales Grade A	£17,900.00
19	Pyrda	Nana	Sales Grade C	£21,200.00
21	Han	Yueng	Sales Grade B	£20,700.00
*	(AutoNumber)			£0.00

FIGURE 3.12 *Result of search for employees earning salary of more than £15,000*

Entering the criterion < "D" in the Surname field in the query returns only those employees whose surname begins with A, B or C, i.e. it comes before D in the alphabet (see Table 3.3).

Complex searches using logical operators

We have discussed the use of logical operators to add precision to searches when using search engines. The same logical operators can be used to search databases on more than one criterion.

In a Microsoft Access® query, entering criteria on the same line is the same as using the AND operator. The query shown in Figure 3.13 is searching for 'position = "cashier" AND contract = "full-time"'. Table 3.4 shows the results of this query.

EMPLOYEE ID	SURNAME	FIRST NAME	POSITION	ANNUAL
9	Croker	Susan	Cashier	£14,500.00
13	Carmody	Marriane	Contractor	
18	Abdullah	Mohammed	Sales Grade	£17,900.00

TABLE 3.3

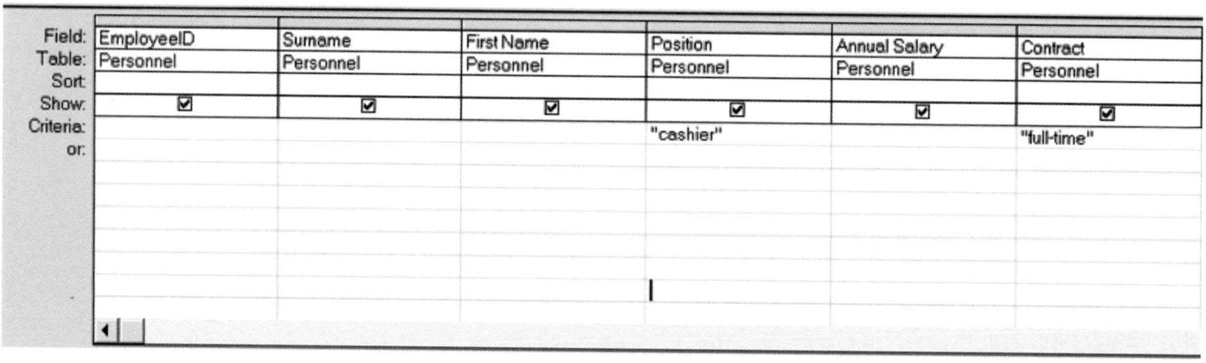

FIGURE 3.13 *A complex search to find cashiers who have a full-time contract*

EMPLOYEE ID	SURNAME	FIRST NAME	POSITION	ANNUAL	CONTRACT
9	Croker	Susan	Cashier	£14,500.00	Full-time
15	Honiker	Samuel	Cashier	£14,500.00	Full-time

TABLE 3.4

The AND operator can be used only with criteria that relate to two or more fields. The OR operator, on the other hand, can be used to select more than one item of data from the same field. In a Microsoft Access® query, entering the criteria on different rows in the query is equivalent to the OR operator. For example, to find employees with the position Sales Grade A OR Sales Grade B requires you to enter "Sales Grade A" and "Sales Grade B" on separate rows in the position column of the query. Table 3.5 shows the results of this query.

Presenting results as a report

The results of the example queries shown so far in this section have been presented as simple tables.

Using database software, it is possible to present the results in a variety of report formats. To do this, you must first create a query; you can then use the query as the information source for the report. The easiest way to create a report is to use the report wizard but you will probably need to make adjustments to the report design in design view.

The report shown in Figure 3.14 is based on the tax code query in Figure 3.10. The report uses a technique called grouping that collects together all the information about, in this case, each position.

EMPLOYEE ID	SURNAME	FIRST NAME	POSITION	ANNUAL	CONTRACT
1	McNamara	Patrick	Sales Grade A	£18,200.00	Full-time
3	Hill	Phyllis	Sales Grade B	£20,000.00	Full-time
8	Ricketts	Diane	Sales Grade A	£17,900.00	Full-time
14	Smith	Anita	Sales Grade A	£17,900.00	Full-time
18	Abdullah	Mohammed	Sales Grade A	£17,900.00	Full-time
21	Han	Yueng	Sales Grade B	£20,700.00	Full-time

TABLE 3.5

Taxcode Query

Position	EmployeeID	Surname	First Name	Annual Salary	N I Number
Cashier					
	9	Croker	Susan	£14,500.00	LD864120V
Contractor					
	17	Nicholls	Amanda		SC567420A
	11	Findlater	Martin		RA890466D
Sales Grade A					
	8	Ricketts	Diane	£17,900.00	GW121905M
Sales Grade B					
	21	Han	Yueng	£20,700.00	HA445890D
	3	Hill	Phyllis	£20,000.00	IJ289001H
Sales Grade C					
	19	Pyrda	Nana	£21,200.00	BA560963D

FIGURE 3.14 *A report based on the tax code query, grouped by position*

Theory into practice

– reports

Practise creating some queries on a local database. Use one of the queries to create a report. First select the *Reports* tab and then select *New*. Use the drop-down list to select a query to create the report from, then select *Report Wizard* and click *Next*. Add the fields that you want to appear in your report by highlighting each one and clicking the right arrow. The double arrow will add all the fields shown to the report. *Next* will move you on to the next screen. If there are records with the same data in one or more fields you can choose to group the data, as in the example. Select the field for grouping and click the right arrow to add it. You can also choose to sort the data. Work through the screens selecting options and finally click *Finish* to see the report. You may find that some field names are not completely visible or that the layout is not easy to read because of the alignment. You can change the layout by selecting *Design View*. Experiment with the layout until you achieve the effect you want. You can keep switching between *Design View* and *Layout Preview* to see the effect of each change.

✳ REMEMBER!

✳ A database is an organised collection of data stored in a computer system.

✳ Databases can be large, small, on-line or stored locally.

✳ Large on-line databases usually have their own search engine or search facility with easy to follow instructions.

✳ Databases can be searched using a single criterion, using relational operators and using logical operators.

✳ If a query is created, this can be used to present the results in a variety of report formats.

Use of spreadsheet facilities

A spreadsheet is a useful tool for analysing and manipulating numerical data. You will need to be able to use a spreadsheet to analyse numerical data you collect, and display the results of this analysis. In order to do that efficiently, you will need to be able to carry out a number of spreadsheet activities independently.

Selecting and setting cell formats to match the data format

The cell format is the way that the data in a cell is displayed. Selecting **Cell** in the **Format** menu will provide a list of the formats available. It is important that the format chosen matches the data in the cell. For example, if the cell contains a number of people, the value will be a whole (or integer) number. However, if a cell contains someone's height in metres, the value will be a decimal number. In the first case it would be pointless to choose a decimal format because the decimal places will always be zero. However, in the second case, if an integer format were chosen, most values would appear simply as 1 or 2 because most people's height is between 1 and 2 metres. The detail of the decimal part of the values would not be displayed – although it would still be stored and used in any calculation. Table 3.6 shows the formats you need to be able to use, typical values and examples of when they should be used.

Selecting and using suitable cell presentation formats

Cell presentation formats allow you to improve the appearance of a spreadsheet to make it easier to read and understand. You need to be able to use all of the following presentation formats effectively.

Horizontal alignment

By default, most spreadsheet packages align text to the left edge of the cell and numbers to the right. The logical values TRUE and FALSE are centred. Whilst this allows for quick differentiation between the two types of data, it does not always make the data as easy to read as it could; for example, when a column heading is left aligned and the numbers below it are aligned to the right. The alignment of any cell can be made left, centred or right. These options can usually be selected using buttons on the toolbar. However, it is not a good idea to centre numerical values, unless they are all single digits, because any sense of place value will be lost.

FORMAT	EXAMPLE	USE
Decimal number	12.34	Values that are not whole numbers.
Integer number	123	Values that are whole numbers.
Percentage	15%	VAT rate, which is entered as 0.175. This cell format will display it as 17.5%
Date	E.g. 03/04/2005, 03-Apr etc.	Any date.
Fraction	E.g. 1/4, 3/10	When you need to display a fraction rather than its decimal equivalent.
Text or character	0123 56789	When you need to treat numbers as text, for example a telephone number – the leading zero would be lost otherwise.
Currency	£123.60	When the values are money.
Scientific	1.23E+06, 1.23E-12	For very large or very small numbers. This uses the form 1.23×10^6, i.e. 1,230,000.
Custom or special	Custom allows you to create your own cell format, while special includes formats such as zip code or telephone number	

TABLE 3.6

Selecting **Cells** from the **Format** menu and then the alignment tab provides additional options. If a cell contains a block of text, it is possible to justify it. This breaks the cell contents into multiple lines within the cell and adjusts the spacing between words so that all lines are as wide as the cell. It is also possible to centre across a selection. This is useful for centring a heading across a number of columns of a spreadsheet. You need to enter the title in the left-most cell. You then select the range of cells and select **Centre across selection**.

Colour

There are a number of ways that colour can be used to enhance the appearance and readability of a spreadsheet. Cells can be filled with colour, and the colour of the cell content can also be changed. Filling different areas of a spreadsheet with different colours can help to differentiate between different parts of the spreadsheet. For example, all cells where the user must enter data can be filled with one colour, while the cells that contain the results of calculations can be filled with another. One convention for showing negative numbers is to display them in red. Care is needed, however, when choosing colours. Red text or numbers on a green background will appear as a brown blur to someone who is red-green colour blind. Too many different colours or colours that clash are more likely to annoy the user than help him or her understand the spreadsheet. One other way that colour can be used is with conditional formatting. This is where the fill colour of a cell can be made to change depending on its content. This is useful to highlight when action is needed, for example when stock levels have fallen below a set value and an order needs to be made.

Vertical alignment

Vertical alignment determines whether the cell content appears at the top of the cell, in the centre or at the bottom. It applies only when a cell is deeper than the height of the characters within it – normally the height of a row automatically adjusts to fit the height of the characters. The vertical alignment options can also be found on the **Alignment** dialog that is accessed by selecting **Cells** from the **Format** menu.

Shading

As well as solid colour fill, there is a range of patterns that can be applied to the cells on a spreadsheet. These can be found by selecting **Cells** from the format menu and then the **Patterns** tab. The colour selected for the cell shading and the pattern must be different or you will simply end up with a solid colour fill. Care is needed when using patterns and shading that any text or numbers in the cells can still be read easily.

Fonts

As with other software packages, when using spreadsheet software you will have access to a wide range of font styles and sizes. Other than for titles or headings, it is best to stick to standard easy-to-read fonts such as Arial or Times New Roman.

> **✳ REMEMBER!**
>
> In a spreadsheet, it is the results that are important. Cell presentation formats should be used to make these easier to understand; fancy fonts may achieve the opposite effect.

Borders

How you use borders will do much to aid the readability of your spreadsheet. A border below the column headings will differentiate them from the data. A border around cells which require data input will make it clear to the user where to enter data, and a border round cells that show the results of calculations will draw attention to them. To apply a border, you select the group of cells and then select **Cells** from the **Format** menu. The **Borders** dialog will allow you to select the type of line you want to use and where you want the border to appear.

Using and manipulating spreadsheet data

Spreadsheet software provides tools that help you to manipulate data. Some of these are similar to those you will be familiar with from using other types of software, such as word processing software. All of these tools can be found in the **Edit** menu.

Find data

Find allows you to locate each occurrence of a particular data item, while **Search** and **Replace** allow you to find particular data items and replace them with something else (see Figure 3.15).

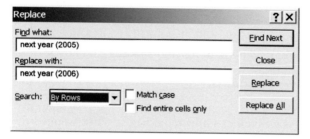

FIGURE 3.15 *Search and Replace dialog*

You can choose to search by row or by column and whether you want to match the case or only match the entire content of a cell. **Find Next** will move to the next occurrence of the data item, which you can then choose to replace or not. **Replace All** will change every occurrence of the data item.

Go to a specified cell

The **Go To** facility is useful if you have a large spreadsheet that is not all visible on-screen. Typing in a cell reference will take you to that cell. What's more, the **Go To** dialog keeps a record of where you started from and any cells you go to, so that you can retrace your steps.

Cut, copy, paste, move

These facilities work in a slightly different way from those in word processing software. When you select a block of cells and select **Cut** the content of the cells does not disappear, but a flashing border appears around it. When you move the cell pointer and select **Paste**, the contents of the original cells will be cleared and will appear in the new location. For the paste facility to work, you must either select exactly the same area of cells as the original, or just a single cell, which will be the top left-hand corner of the new block of cells.

Copy works in the same way, but the content of the original cells is not cleared. If you want to paste the cut or copied cells within the area of the spreadsheet that contains data, rather than **Paste** you can use **Insert Copied Cells**. This works best

with a whole row or column. It is also possible to move the content of cells by selecting the cell(s) and dragging them to a new position on the spreadsheet.

Clear cell formats/contents

If you select a cell and press the delete key on the keyboard, it will clear the contents of the cell but leave any formatting intact. By selecting **Clear** in the **Edit** menu, you can choose whether you want to clear everything from the cell, the formatting, the content or just a comment that is attached to it.

Use paste special

Paste special allows you to choose what you want to paste. For example, if you are pasting values that are the results of calculations to somewhere else on the spreadsheet, or to another spreadsheet, you need to use paste special and paste the values. If you paste the formulae, the cell references may not be correct and you will get error messages or different values from what you expect.

Using cell referencing facilities appropriately

These are the facilities that allow you to perform calculations on the data in a spreadsheet so that you can obtain useful results. Cell referencing allows you to include the contents of particular cells in a formula or function. This is what allows results to be recalculated if the values in the cells are changed.

Cell referencing

Most cell referencing used in formulae is relative cell referencing. This means that if the formula is copied down a column of cells, the cell references change to match, as shown in Table 3.7.

	A	B	C
1			=A1+B1
2			=A2+B2
3			=A3+B3

TABLE 3.7

	A	B	C	D	E	F	G	H
1	Hourly rate	£8.50						
2			Hours worked					
3			Week 1	Week 2	Week 3	Week 4	Total Hours	Wages
4		Maggie	36	29	40	27	132	£1,122.00
5		Deepak	25	30	29	44	128	£1,088.00
6		Surinder	28	31	29	40	128	£1,088.00
7		Judith	15	20	17	12	64	£544.00
8		John	25	36	29	26	116	£986.00

TABLE 3.8

Absolute cell referencing is used when you want to always use the value in a particular cell in a formula. An example of this would be the hourly rate in the example shown in Table 3.8.

The wages for each member of staff are calculated by multiplying their total hours by the hourly rate. The formula in cell H4 is =G4*B1. The $ symbols show that this is an absolute cell reference. To make a cell reference absolute, you move the cell pointer onto that cell so that it appears in the formula and then press F4 on the keyboard. When the formula is copied into cells H5 to H8, the first cell reference will change but B1 will stay the same. So the formula in H8 will be =G8*B1. The advantage of this is that, if the hourly rate changes or you want to see the effect of changing it, only one value needs to be changed in the spreadsheet. Mixed referencing is when either the row or the column is absolute and the other is relative, for example B$2 or B2$.

Another way of achieving the same thing is to name the cell. Select the cell, then select **Name** in the **Insert** menu. You then select **Define**. If there is a label next to the cell to say what it contains, use this to name the cell. Otherwise, you can type a name in. The name can then be used in formulae, rather than an absolute reference. It is also possible to name a *range of cells*.

A spreadsheet workbook can consist of a number of linked worksheets. You can reference cells on different sheets in a formula. This is known as 3D referencing. This will appear as, for example, =Sheet1!B2.

All the references so far have involved columns labelled with letters A, B, C, etc. and rows labelled with numbers. There is another method of referencing where both the columns and rows are numbered. This is usually referred to as R1C1 referencing. In this case, the row number comes first, followed by the column number. The way that relative and absolute referencing appears is also different. Using the previous example, the formula for wages will appear as =R1C2*RC[-1]. R1C1 denotes an absolute reference to that cell. RC[-1] indicates that the formula should use the value in the cell in the same row, one column to the left.

Formulae

Operators are used with cell references to create formulae. When describing cell referencing we have used the arithmetic operators + (add)

OPERATOR	EXAMPLE	WHAT IT DOES
+	A1+A2	Adds the contents of the two cells together
-	A1−A2	Subtracts the contents of A2 from that of A1
*	A1*A2	Multiplies the content of the two cells together
/	A1/A2	Divides the content of A1 by the content of A2
%	A1/A2%	Divides the content of A1 by the content of A2 then multiplies the answer by 100 to give it as a percentage
^	A1^3	Raises the content of A1 to the power 3, i.e. A1*A1*A1

TABLE 3.9

and * (multiply). A list of other arithmetic operators that you need to be able to use are listed in Table 3.9.

Text as well as numbers can be added using &. This is called concatenation. If A1 contains 'red' and B1 contains 'hat', =A1&B1 will give 'redhat'.

It is also possible to use relational operators in formulae. This can test whether the relationship is true or false. The result of this will be the logical value TRUE if the relationship is true or the logical value FALSE if it is not. This is best demonstrated using an example (see Table 3.10).

Obviously, you don't need a formula to tell you that 25 is not equal to 30 but these relational operators can be used to compare the results of other calculations.

As with any mathematics, there is an order or precedence for operators. The order in which operations will be evaluated is %, ^, * and /, + and −, & and then the relational operators = < > <= >= <>. You can change the order by using brackets, more correctly called parentheses. Whatever is in the brackets will be evaluated first. This is best shown by an example using simple numbers. The sum 2+3*4 will give the answer 14. The multiplication is done first 3*4=12 − and then the 2 is added to give 14. However, using parentheses (2+3)*4 will give an answer of 20. The bracket is evaluated first to give 5, which is then multiplied by 4 to give 20. When you are creating formulae in a spreadsheet you need to take great care over the order of precedence and use parentheses when necessary. If you do not, you may find the results of calculations are not what you expected.

A1	B1	FORMULA	RELATIONSHIP	RESULT
25	30	=A1=B1	Is equal to	FALSE
25	30	=A1>B1	Is greater than	FALSE
25	30	=A1<B1	Is less than	TRUE
25	30	=A1>=B1	Is greater than or equal to	FALSE
25	30	=A1<=B1	Is less than or equal to	TRUE
25	30	=A1<>B1	Is not equal to	TRUE

TABLE 3.10

FUNCTION	EXAMPLE	WHAT IT DOES
SUM	=SUM(A1:A6)	Adds the values in the range of cells from A1 to A6
INT	=INT(A1/A2)	Rounds the answer of A1/A2 to the nearest whole number (integer)
COUNT	=COUNT(A1:C6)	Counts how many cells in the range contain numbers
MAX	=MAX(A1:A6)	Finds the highest value in the range A1 to A6
AVERAGE	=AVERAGE(A1:A6)	Calculates the mathematical mean or average of the values in the range A1 to A6
RAND	=RAND()*100	Generates a random number between 0 and 1 that can then be multiplied by 100 to give a value between 1 and 100
	=INT(RAND()*100)	Adding the INT function will give a whole number between 1 and 100
MODE	=MODE(A1:A6)	Finds the modal (most common) value in the range of cells
MIN	=MIN(A1:A6)	Finds the lowest value in the range A1 to A6
SQUARE	=SQUARE(A1)	Calculates the square root of the value in A1
IF	=IF(A1>A2, Profit, Loss)	If the value of A1 is greater than that of A2, the cell will display the word Profit, otherwise it will display the word Loss. The format is: IF(condition, what to do if TRUE, what to do if FALSE)
MEDIAN	=MEDIAN(A1:A6)	Returns the middle value in the range A1 to A6
DATE	=DATE(2005,02,27)	Returns the number that represents the date

TABLE 3.11

Functions

As well as using operators in formulae you create, spreadsheet software offers a range of built-in functions that you can use. Table 3.11 shows the functions you should be able to use, with an example and what it does.

Wizards

Microsoft Excel provides some wizards to help build more complex formulae. For example, if you wanted to find the value where a particular row and column intersect, you can use the lookup wizard. As with any wizard, you will be taken through the process step by step. You just need to follow the instructions carefully to create the formula.

how much of that time they spend on different activities each week; for example, using the Internet, other computer use, watching television, physical activity, etc. Record the age range, gender and occupation of each person, the hours of leisure time and the hours spent on each activity. Enter the data in a spreadsheet. Calculate the time spent on each activity as a percentage of the leisure time available. Find the maximum, minimum and average time spent on each activity for a particular age group. Do the same for a particular gender or occupation. Use cell presentation formats to make the spreadsheet easy to follow. You may need to copy data onto different worksheets to analyse the data in different ways.

Development of spreadsheets to present results of data analysis

As part of the assessment evidence for this unit you will need to use a spreadsheet to analyse numerical data and present the results. This may be data that you have collected or it may be numerical data you have found on the Internet, such as census data or other statistics. The Office of National Statistics' website, for example, provides data sets on a wide range of topic areas that can be downloaded but you may also find numerical data from many other sources.

The spreadsheet in Figure 3.16 shows how you can use the facilities available to improve the presentation of data. The original data had each year's figures beneath one another in a single column with a blank row between each year and

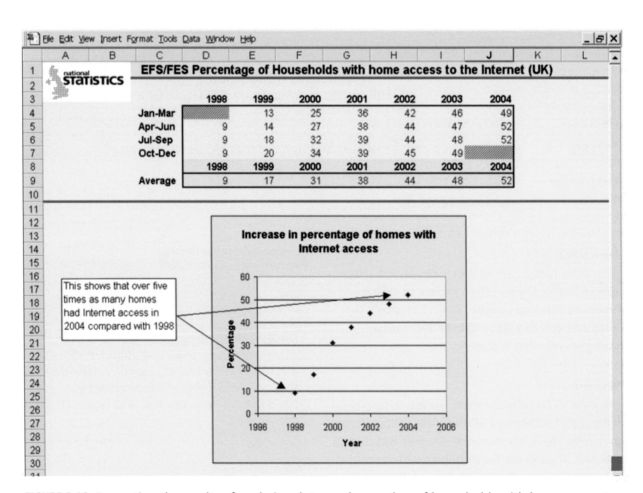

FIGURE 3.16 *Presenting the results of analysing data on the number of households with home access to the Internet (Source: Office of National Statistics)*

the next. Whilst this showed the increase quite well, it was not easy to view as the figures did not all fit on the screen and you had to scroll down to see them. It was also not clear, without looking closely, that there were only three quarters' figures for the first and last year. The data has been moved so that the years are the column headings and the quarters the row headings. The average value has been taken for each year using the AVERAGE function. As this gave decimal values for some years, INT was used as well to give whole number values, i.e. =INT(AVERAGE( )). Additional columns were added to the left so that the table is in the centre of the screen and the font size of the title has been increased and centred across the cells. Finally, the year column headings have been copied to the row above the averages, so that the two rows can be used in a chart.

To improve the appearance, two colours have been used, with borders to separate the title from the data and the data from the chart. Borders have also been added around the data and to highlight the average values. The cells for the quarters with no data have also been shaded. The years and average figures have been used to create and insert a chart – an x-y plot. This has been resized to fit the space available and so that the increase is shown clearly. The two rows of data used have been highlighted in green to link them to the chart. The Office of National Statistics' logo has been copied from the website and added in the top left-hand corner to indicate where the data was obtained, and a text box and arrows were added using the drawing toolbar.

Cell formatting

You should already be familiar with the cell formatting facilities and those for manipulating the spreadsheet from the previous section. We will now consider the other facilities used in this example in more detail.

Drawing tools and graphic images

Spreadsheet software, such as Microsoft Excel, provides the same drawing toolbar as other packages. This means that you can add shapes, lines, arrows, text boxes and WordArt to your spreadsheet. You will also be able to group drawn

objects and move or copy them as one, align objects with each other or change the way objects are layered. You may have used these facilities in your work for Unit 1: Using ICT to communicate, so we will not explain again how to use them here. As with all presentation techniques, you need to take care how such objects are used – they should enhance the information in the spreadsheet, not detract from it.

As in the example, you can also add graphic images to a spreadsheet. This may be a logo, or some other images that illustrate the information being presented. Choosing **Picture** from the **Insert** menu will give you the option of using clipart or a picture from file. In either case, when you have found the image you want, it will appear on the spreadsheet and you can resize or position it as you want.

Charts and line graphs

Charts and graphs are an excellent way of showing statistical information so that it can be grasped quickly. The chart in Figure 3.16 shows very clearly how the number of households with home access to the Internet has increased. If you are going to create a chart, you need to ensure that the data is arranged appropriately. Sometimes it may be necessary to copy column or row headings and values to another part of the spreadsheet so that you can select the data you want to graph (hence the need to copy the year headings in the previous example).

Table 3.12 shows more data on Internet access from the Office of National Statistics' website. We will use this to demonstrate how to create a multiple line graph to compare the increase in home Internet access for different income bands. First you need to select the data, together with the row and column headings, that you want to graph. This will exclude the title row and the bottom row of data, but include all the rest. You then select **Chart** from the **Insert** menu (or click the chart button on the toolbar). This will open the **Chart Wizard** that will help you create the graph. Your first task is to select the type of chart. Care is needed here. The type of chart you choose must match the purpose. For example, a pie chart would show clearly the percentages for different

HOUSEHOLDS WITH HOME ACCESS TO THE INTERNET BY GROSS INCOME DECILE GROUP (UK)						
	1998–99	1999–00	2000–01	2001–02	2002–03	2003–04
Lowest 10%	3	6	7	10	12	15
Second decile group	1	3	5	12	14	15
Third decile group	2	4	12	15	22	20
Fourth decile group	3	6	17	25	30	37
Fifth decile group	4	15	26	33	41	41
Sixth decile group	7	15	32	43	48	55
Seventh decile group	10	22	43	49	56	60
Eighth decile group	16	28	49	59	68	71
Ninth decile group	19	38	60	67	74	78
Highest decile group	32	48	73	80	85	89
All households	10	19	32	39	45	48

TABLE 3.12

income groups in a particular year, but would not be any use for demonstrating the increase for a particular group. In this case we are going to select the line option. This will give further options of how the lines will be displayed and whether the row or column headings will be used on the x-axis. There is a button that you can press and hold to see how each option will display the data. The default option is fine in this case so we press **Next** to move to the next screen. On this screen we need to check that the dates are on the x-axis by selecting the rows radio button. The next screen is one of the most important. It gives you the opportunity to enter a title and labels for the axes. A chart or graph is meaningless if it is not properly labelled. You can also add or remove grid lines and decide where any legend (key) will appear. If you are using only one data series (one row or column of data) in your chart, make sure you uncheck the show legend box. The final screen allows you to choose whether you want the chart to appear on the same worksheet as the data, as in the first example, or on a new worksheet. In this instance we will choose a new sheet. The result is shown in Figure 3.17.

Hopefully, this shows at a glance that the increase for the higher income groups has been greater than for those in the lower income bands – as we mentioned earlier in this unit.

Using macros

A macro is a series of instructions that is defined as a single element. The easiest way to create macros is to record them. Each macro can then be assigned to a key combination or a button. Running the macro repeats the steps that were recorded.

To record a macro, you select **Macro** from the **Tools** menu and then **Record** new macro. You will be asked to give the macro a name. You will also have the option of assigning a shortcut key and deciding where the macro is stored – this will determine where it can be used. Next you carry out the steps that you want the macro to perform and, when you have finished, you click the **Stop** recording button.

The next stage is to create a button on the spreadsheet to activate the macro. You can do this using the drawing toolbar. Draw a rectangle or other suitable shape in an appropriate position on the spreadsheet. Right-clicking on the shape will

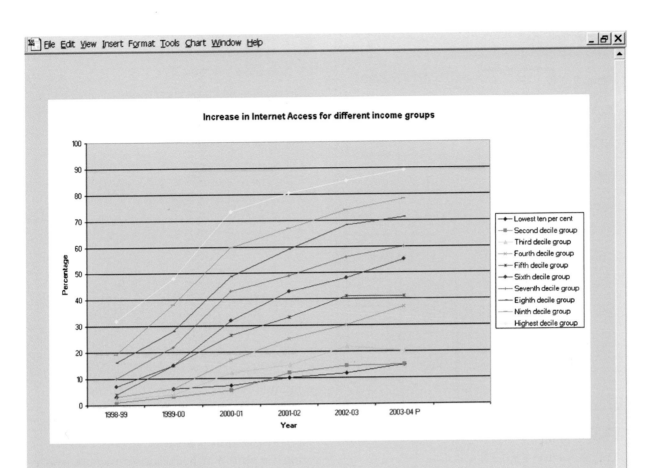

Increase in Internet Access for different income groups

Percentage

Year

Legend:
- Lowest ten per cent
- Second decile group
- Third decile group
- Fourth decile group
- Fifth decile group
- Sixth decile group
- Seventh decile group
- Eighth decile group
- Ninth decile group
- Highest decile group

FIGURE 3.17 *Line graph to show the increase in the number of households with home Internet access for different income groups (Source: Office of National Statistics)*

bring up a menu of options. This will allow you to add text to the shape, format the shape and, most importantly, assign a macro to it. When you have finished formatting your button, clicking elsewhere on the spreadsheet will get rid of the menu. Now if you move the mouse pointer over your button, it will change to a hand. Clicking on the button will activate the macro.

There are several reasons for using macros. The most obvious is when an action requires you to make a number of key depressions or mouse clicks. This might be used, for example, if you need to copy the results from one worksheet into another, or if you want to clear the data content of all the cells in a spreadsheet ready for new data. You can also use a macro to bring up a form like that shown in Figure 3.18 that allows you to enter data a record at a time, rather than directly into the rows in the spreadsheet.

The **Form** option is in the **Data** menu. Each new record entered will appear on the next empty row of the spreadsheet. You can also scroll through the records and edit them. Another use for a macro is to print out a report, or to move to the worksheet that will show the report on-screen, perhaps changing the view to full screen so that all the toolbars, etc. are removed and there is the maximum area to show the results. In all cases, you can create the macros by recording the steps needed and then assigning the macro to a drawing object with a suitable text label.

Testing

Any spreadsheet you create to analyse and present data will be of little use if the results produced are not accurate. As well as ensuring that you enter the data accurately, you also need

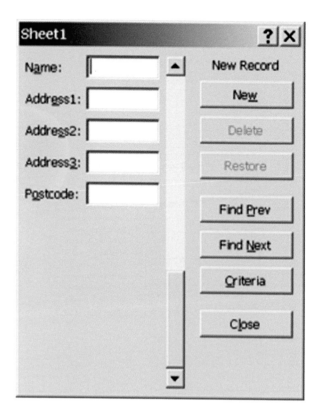

FIGURE 3.18 *A simple data entry form*

Presentation of the results of an investigation

In this section of the unit, you will need to use the skills described in Unit 1: Using ICT to communicate. In particular, you will need to combine different types of information into a coherent presentation. This may, for example, be a slide presentation, website or an on-screen or printed report. Whichever format you use, you need to make sure that different elements work together, rather than simply throw them together. You will need to include:

* text from existing sources as well as text you create yourself. You may need to edit or rephrase the text you use to ensure that there is a consistent writing style

* graphics, numerical spreadsheet data, graphs and charts and the results of database searches should all be incorporated so that it is clear why they are there. They should be clearly labelled, referred to in the text and positioned near the text they refer to. In some cases, it might be better to include the numerical data or database search results in a clearly labelled and referenced appendix, rather than in the body of the presentation

* if your presentation is on-screen, you will be able to incorporate hyperlinks to other information sources, either stored locally or on the WWW. Such links should be used with care. The additional information needs to be relevant to your presentation and be useful to the reader.

to test that the formulae you use generate the results you expect. There are several ways of doing this. You can estimate the range that results should be within and check that the actual result is within that range. For example, the average of a set of figures should be within the range of the values in the set. If the result is outside this range, there is likely to be an error in the formula. Similarly, if you estimate the result as being less than 100 and the result given is over 1000, an error in the formula is the most likely cause.

Another way of testing that the formulae in your spreadsheet do what they should is to use dummy data. In other words, use simple numbers for which you can easily work out the expected results. If the actual results are different, this will highlight any errors in the formulae. The final way of testing the formulae is to use a calculator or pencil and paper to work out what the results should be and then compare these with the actual results.

Accuracy and currency of information

As has been mentioned previously, anyone can create a website and display information on the WWW. Also, websites can easily become out of date – sites are rarely deleted when the person who created them loses interest and stops updating them. This means that you need to take steps to check the accuracy of any information you find and how up to date the information is.

The best way to check that information is accurate is to compare information from more than one source. If you find that two sources give different information about the same topic, you will need to look at more sources to help you determine which is accurate or to come to a consensus. The different sources may be other websites, or they may be books or other paper-based sources.

To check whether information is up to date, you need to try to find when it was last updated. Some sites, but not all, will display this information. Do not be fooled by the fact that the current date is displayed on the page. This just means that the page includes a today's date field. One way of ensuring that you download only up-to-date information is to use the 'last updated' feature in the advanced search facility of the search engine.

If you are using information from government or other large public-service websites, it is to be hoped that the information is accurate and up to date.

Acknowledging sources

When you collect and use information, it is very important that you acknowledge the sources of the information you use. You will need to list all of your sources accurately so that someone else can find the original information and check that they agree with your interpretation of it. You will also need to acknowledge the owner of the copyright of any graphics or other material you include in your presentation. An important part of presenting your results will, therefore, be a *bibliography*. You may also want to use footnotes to reference the sources of particular items.

> **Key term**
>
> *Bibliography*: list of sources used in a presentation or report.

Assessment evidence

A local retailer is considering selling goods on the Internet using e-commerce and communicating with its customers only by email. You have been asked to investigate what e-commerce might involve and the impact that relying solely on electronic communication methods might have. You need to present the results of your investigation, including the use of a spreadsheet to analyse numerical data, in an appropriate way. You also need to produce a report on the sources and methods that you used to find the information. This should include screen prints to show the methods you used. To produce the presentation and report you will need to carry out the following linked tasks.

Task A

Select and use search engines to find information on the WWW.

As a minimum you will need to identify the information you need, choose a search engine and use standard search facilities to find the information. If you use the advanced search facilities of more than one search engine and compare the results you will reach mark band two. To reach mark band three you will need to choose the most appropriate search engine and use efficient methods, including using logical operators to find the information.

Task B

Explain the impact of the availability of electronic information on individuals and society. You need to consider this in the context of the assignment as well as in general terms and use the information you collect and the results of analysing that information to aid your explanation.

As a minimum you need to make straightforward comments on how the availability of information affects people you are familiar with. If you can extend this to give a clear explanation that includes society in general and people and situations outside your normal experience you will be able to reach mark band two. To reach mark band three you will need to explain in detail how organisations communicate with individuals and society and how this affects those who don't have (or want) access to ICT.

This task will be used to assess the quality of your written communication so you should ensure that your report is well structured and contains few, if any, errors in spelling, grammar and punctuation.

Task C

Access information from large public-service websites.

If you need some help to find the information you need, you will reach only mark band one. To reach mark band two you will need to be able to find the information without help using menus, navigation bars, alphabetical indexes and textual hyperlinks. If you can also use an internal search engine you will be able to reach mark band three.

Task D

Use databases to find information.

As a minimum you must use search criteria that involve relational operators to get information from at least one database, either local or on-line. If you can use complex search criteria that also involve logical operators, get information from both local and on-line databases and present the results, for example in a table, you will achieve mark band two. To reach the highest mark band, you must also be able to present your results as reports.

Task E

Use spreadsheet software to analyse numerical data and present results. You could, for example, find data on Internet access and individuals' use of on-line shopping on the WWW. You could also carry out a survey to find similar information for your local area and compare the results.

As a minimum, you must create a suitable spreadsheet layout and use it to carry out simple analysis of the data. You must present the output on screen or on paper and use cell formats, charts

or graphs, page or screen layout and graphic images appropriately. If you are able to carry out more complex analysis that shows you have a good understanding of spreadsheet formulae and functions and use macros to speed up data input and the production of results, you will reach mark band two. To reach mark band three, your spreadsheet must be well designed and you must test it thoroughly to make sure your results are accurate.

Task F

Combine different types of data to present the results of your investigation.

As a minimum your report must combine at least two different types of data from a small number of sources (2 or 3). You must also list the sources you use. To reach mark band two your report must combine at least three different types of data from a number of different sources (4 to 6) and you must list the sources appropriately. There should be enough detail for someone else to find the information. To reach the highest mark band, your presentation must be well thought out and coherent. You must combine a range of data from a wide range of sources (more than 6) and list your sources in a detailed bibliography.

Task G

Evaluate the methods you used to find information and present results.
You need to consider:

* what worked well – what was good about the methods you used

* what did not work – what was not so good

* how well did your methods achieve the required results?

* how did you refine your initial methods to meet the purpose more closely?

* how would you improve the methods you used if you had to do a similar task in the future?

As a minimum you must comment on how effective the methods you used were for finding the information and presenting results. If you clearly identify good and not so good features of the methods you used, you will reach mark band two. To reach the highest mark band you must show that you have identified strengths and weaknesses in the methods you used originally and how you refined these methods to meet the purpose more closely. You must also suggest how you might approach a similar task in future.

Signposting for portfolio evidence

In this assignment, the methods you use to find and analyse information are as important as the content of the presentation. As well as the presentation itself, you will need to make sure that you provide screen prints to show the search methods you have used and evidence of how you created and tested your spreadsheet. For example, you should include a formula printout. Currently, all of your evidence must be produced on paper. If you have created a screen-based presentation, you will need to provide screen prints or printouts to evidence your work. You will need to annotate these to indicate any features, such as animation or hyperlinks that are not obvious from the printouts. You should get your teacher to witness these features and initial or sign the printouts to confirm that the features work. For example, printing out a slide presentation as an audience handout with three slides to a page will provide space for you to add any necessary annotations.

You need to organise your work carefully. Make sure each piece of work is clearly labelled to show what it is and that your name is on each page. Put your work in a logical order. This might be your report on how you found the information and analysed it, followed by your presentation, with your evaluation at the end. Alternatively, you may consider the report to be most important and put that first. When you have put all your work in a sensible order, number all the pages and create a contents page to show where each piece of work is located.

GLOSSARY

Appendix
Numbered sections at the end of a document that contain relevant information referred to in the document but not part of it.

Assets
Anything of monetary value that is owned by an organisation.

BACS (Banks Automated Clearing System)
A system that transfers money electronically from one bank account to another.

Balance sheet
A financial statement that lists the assets of an organisation.

Bandwidth
The number of bits per second that can be transmitted.

Batch processing
Processing where all the data is collected or input and then all the records are processed in a single operation.

Bespoke software
Software specially designed and written for an organisation.

Bitmap images
Images that are made up of a two-dimensional array of dots or pixels, each of which corresponds to one or more bits in the computer's memory.

Browser software
Software that allows you to access and view web pages.

Cash flow
A measure of the money coming into and going out of the organisation, usually on a monthly basis.

Commercial organisation
An organisation that sells products or services in order to make a profit.

Computer viruses
Small computer programs that can copy themselves from one computer to another and that are almost always written to cause damage to the computers they infect.

Curriculum vitae (cv)
A document that includes your personal details and your education and employment history (called a resume in the US).

Data controller
The person(s) who determines the how and for what purpose personal data will be used.

Data subjects
The individuals whose information is stored and processed.

Database
An organised collection of data stored in a computer system.

Department
A group of people performing a particular job function under the direction of a department manager.

Design brief
A summary of the specification of a product or service.

Digital television broadcasting
Transmits multimedia data in streamed bits (binary digit, i.e. 0 or 1) of data.

Direct marketing
Sending marketing information directly to a list of potential customers.

Electronic data interchange (EDI)
The exchange of standardised document forms between computer systems for business use.

Email
Written information that is communicated electronically.

Employees
The people who work for and are employed by an organisation.

Encryption key
Key needed to unscramble encrytped data so that it is meaningful

Encryption
A security method that involves scrambling information transmitted so that it cannot be read if it is intercepted.

Flat-file database
A database consisting of a single table of data.

Font
Typeface.

Frequency
The particular waveband at which radio signals are broadcast or transmitted.

Gutter
The blank area of margin on the inside edge of pages that are to be bound that will be within the binding.

Hyperlink
An area of an on-screen document or presentation that takes the user to another part of the presentation or to a different location, such as another file or a web page, when it is clicked on.

Internet
A world-wide network of computer networks.

Invoice
A document that lists the products or services purchased from an organisation together with the cost of each, any additional costs such as carriage, the VAT due and the total amount to be paid.

Job functions
Staff who are responsible for carrying out specific tasks within an organisation, such as sales or finance.

Media
Medium used to express or communicate information.

Multimedia
Using more than one medium to express or communicate information.

Optical storage medium
A disk that stores data by altering the optical characteristics of the surface material, e.g. the way light is reflected off it.

Orphan
Where the last line of a paragraph ends up on its own at the top of a new page.

PDA (personal digital assistant)
A handheld computer that provides facilities for maintaining a diary, address book, notebook etc.

Permanent contracts
Employment contracts that have no end date.

Personal data
Data that relates to a living individual who can be identified from the data on its own or from the data along with other information held.

Premium
The amount of money you pay to an insurance company to provide insurance cover.

Profit and loss statements
List the income and expenditure of an organisation.

Purchase ledger
The section of the accounts system that keeps records of all the purchases made by the organisation and the money paid out for these purchases.

Purchase orders
Documents that list the goods or services that an organisation wants to purchase from a supplier.

Questionnaire
A document designed to gather information and opinions from large numbers of individuals, often as part of a survey or to gain feedback on services provided

Quotation
Details of what a product or service will cost.

Range of cells
A block of cells that is defined by the addresses of the top-left and bottom-right cells.

Report
A long document that presents the results of some research or the activities an organisation has undertaken during the previous year and its financial position

Robotics
Computer controlled devices that are able to carry out tasks that would have previously been done by people.

Sales ledger
The section of the accounts system that keeps records of the sales made by the organisation and the money paid in for the goods or services sold.

Search engines
Computer programs that search a database to find the information required, either within a website or on the WWW.

Set-top box
A box about the size of a DVD player that is connected between the satellite dish, aerial or cable input and the television set.

Short-term fixed contracts
Employment contracts that last for a specified time, for example one year.

SMS (short message service)
Telephone text messaging

Spreadsheet
A tool for analysing and manipulating numerical data.

Staff development plan
A document that identifies the existing knowledge and skills of employees and how these can be extended and updated to improve performance.

Tax code
A code issued by the Inland Revenue and based on each individual's personal circumstances that is used to calculate how much income tax should be deducted from their wages or salary.

Telesales
Selling goods or services by taking orders over the telephone.

Template
A template allows you to set the style and size of fonts and the position of items so that these are the same in every document.

Textual hotspots
Words within a web page that, when clicked on, take you to another part of the site, or even to an external site

Touch screen

Screens that allow people to interact with a computer without the need for a keyboard, mouse or other input device.

URL

Uniform Resource Locator – the unique address of the page on the Internet.

Utility companies

Companies that provide utilities such as water, electricity, gas and telephone services.

Vector graphic

Images that are made up of simple geometric shapes. Geometric information is stored, such as the co-ordinates of the start and end point of a straight line.

WAP

Wireless application protocol.

Web browser

Software that allows you to view web pages. The most common is Internet Explorer.

Widow

Where the first line of a paragraph is left on its own at the bottom of a page.

Working practices

The way that work is organised and carried out.

INDEX

Double up!

Thinking of taking the AS Level GCE Applied ICT double award?

Help is on hand once again from Heinemann.

AS Level GCE Applied ICT Double Award for OCR

Get the book to match your exact needs for the OCR Double Award.

- Case studies and activities link the theory to real IT industry practices to make it easy to understand.

- Tips and suggestions throughout help you to achieve success.

- Covers all the units you need to get your double award.

AS Level ICT Double Award, for OCR
0 435 44996 6   £19.99

Series Editor: Mary Reid

UNITS COVERED

- Using ICT to Communicate
- How Organisations use ICT
- ICT Solutions for Individuals and Society
- System Specification and Configuration
- Problem Solving using ICT
- Software Development – Design
- Communications Technologies
- Introduction to Programming

Have your say!

We love to hear what you think about our books. Did you know that you can post your comments about this book on our website? Visit www.heinemann.co.uk/vocational to find this book, and click on 'submit review'. It's that simple.

Authors

Maggie Banks	Sonia Stuart
Glen Millbery	Karen Scott

Find out more!

Visit your local bookshop or call our Customer Services Department quoting the following promotional code – F 666 ICT 08.

t 01865 888068 **f** 01865 314029 **e** orders@heinemann.co.uk **w** www.heinemann.co.uk

Heinemann
Inspiring generations